ALASKA

THE LAND · THE PEOPLE · THE CITIES

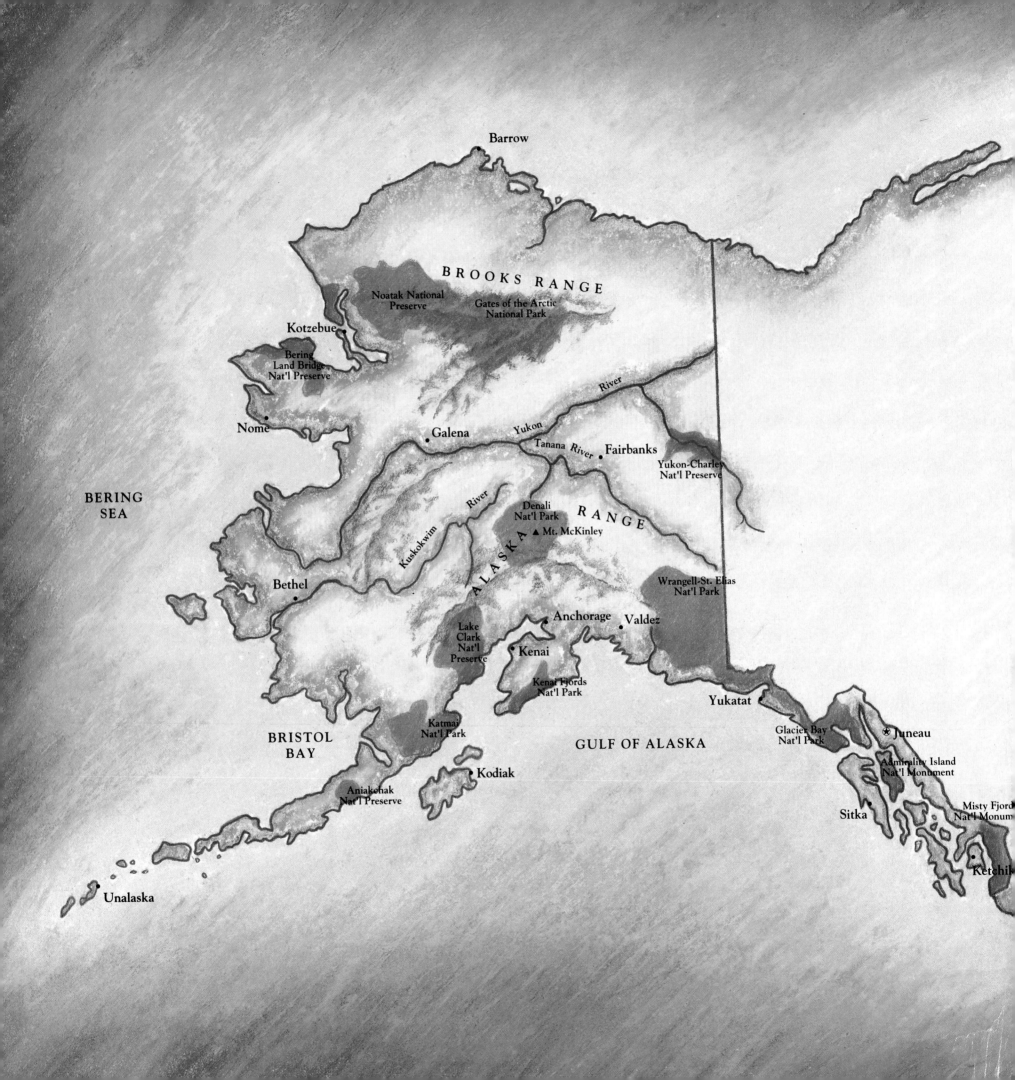

ALASKA

THE LAND · THE PEOPLE · THE CITIES

MICHAEL MACY

MALLARD PRESS

MALLARD PRESS

AN IMPRINT OF BDD PROMOTIONAL BOOK COMPANY, INC.

666 FIFTH AVENUE · NEW YORK · NEW YORK 10103

A FRIEDMAN GROUP BOOK
Published by MALLARD PRESS
An imprint of BDD Promotional Book Company, Inc.
666 Fifth Avenue
New York, New York 10103

Mallard Press and its accompanying design and logo are trademarks of
BDD Promotional Book Company, Inc.

ISBN 0-7924-5295-X

ALASKA
The Land, The People, The Cities
was prepared and produced by
Michael Friedman Publishing Group, Inc.
15 West 26th Street
New York, New York 10010

Editor: Sharyn Rosart
Designer: Stephanie Bart-Horvath
Photo Editor: Ede Rothaus

Typset by The Interface Group, Inc.
Color separations by United South Seas Graphic Art Co., Inc.
Printed and bound in Hong Kong by Leefung-Asco Printers, Ltd.

This book is dedicated to Alaska, her residents,
admirers, and protectors, on the occasion of the
250th anniversary of her discovery by Europeans.

Acknowledgments

The author would like to thank Kay Shelton, India Spartz, and the rest of the staff of the Alaska State Historical Library for their assistance. Steve Henrikson at the Alaska State Museum was kind enough to assemble and provide a selection of slides and background documentation on Alaska Native artifacts from the Museum's collection. Similarly, Acting Chief Park Ranger Cicely Muldoon of the Sitka National Historic Park and her assistants provided slides and background information on their collection of totem poles. Finally, Sharyn Rosart and Ede Rothaus of Michael Friedman Publishing Group proved to be most capable and understanding editors.

CONTENTS

THE LAND

Where exactly is Alaska? The northernmost state is roughly equidistant from Japan, Europe, and the east coast of North America. Jets flying polar routes between these regions refuel in Anchorage, Alaska, which is why residents of Anchorage call their city "the crossroads of the world". Alaska is actually closer to Siberia than it is to Washington State. There are 500 miles (800 km) of Canadian coastline between Ketchikan, Alaska's southernmost city, and Seattle, Washington, but only 51 miles (80 km) of the Bering Strait separate Cape Prince of Wales on the Alaskan mainland from the Siberian mainland. Little Diomede Island, U.S.A., lies a mere 3 miles (5 km) from Big Diomede Island, U.S.S.R. Barrow, Alaska's northernmost community, is closer to the North Pole, a mere 800 miles (1,300 km), than it is to Juneau, the state capital. On the east, for more than 1,200 miles (1,800 km), Alaska abuts Canada's province of British Columbia and Yukon Territory.

SUNSET LIGHTS THE treacherous waters and quick-mud flats near Girdwood on the upper reaches of Turnagain Arm.

Geography

By any measure, Alaska is big; in fact, it is one-fifth the size of the rest of the country. The state covers some 586,412 square miles (1,524,671 km²), more land than the combined area of the next three largest states. Its coastline runs for 6,540 miles (10,464 km). Alaska's 33,904-mile (54,246-km) shoreline (which includes the state's many islands) exceeds the combined total of the other forty-nine states. Alaska borders two oceans, the North Pacific and the Arctic, and three seas, the Beaufort, Bering, and Chukchi.

Alaska is so big that it is often subdivided into six distinct regions. These subdivisions make it easier to picture and understand the state.

SOUTHEAST consists of a narrow slice of the mainland and the Alexander Archipelago, the islands north and west of British Columbia. On the map, Southeast Alaska looks like a small appendage, an afterthought, but it is 125 miles (200 km) wide and 450 miles (720 km) long. Most famous of its myriad waterways is the Inside Passage.

COTTONWOOD, ASPEN, and birch ablaze among spruce in early September in the Alaska Range near the entrance to Denali National Park.

SOUTHCENTRAL includes the Chugach Mountains, Copper River Valley and Delta, Prince William Sound, Kenai Peninsula, Kodiak Island, Matanuska and Susitna basins, and the south slope of the Alaska Range.

INTERIOR (formerly called Central) includes the Tanana and Koyukuk basins and all other drainages of the Yukon River system west of the Canadian border, north of the crest of the Alaska Range and south of the crest of the Brooks Range.

ARCTIC extends from the Yukon border west along the north slope of the Brooks Range to Cape Lisburne.

NORTHWEST consists of those areas north and west of the lower Yukon River. This includes the Kobuk and Noatak river drainages, Kotzebue Sound, Seward Peninsula, Norton Sound, and Nunivak and St. Lawrence Islands.

SOUTHWEST is the region that covers the Kuskokwim River drainage, the Bristol Bay drainages, the Alaska Peninsula, and the Aleutian Chain.

MUSKEG POND,
Glacier Bay.

DWARF FIREWEED (EPILOBIUM LATIFOLIUM) COLONIZES RECENTLY
disturbed sites such as roadsides and river bars, paving the way for other species.
Sprouting from seeds borne on wind and water, these add color to an otherwise drab
gravel bar, typical of the Coast ranges.

ALASKAN SUPERLATIVES

Not surprisingly, an area as large as Alaska is home to many geographical superlatives. Denali, or Mount McKinley, is North America's highest peak, at 20,320 feet (6,096 m). Alaska also boasts the eleven highest U.S. peaks, and Kodiak, the largest island in the United States. Alaska has three million lakes larger than 20 acres (8 ha) and three thousand rivers. At 1,000 square miles, (2,600 km^2), Lake Iliamna is North America's second largest freshwater lake. The Yukon River runs for 1,875 miles (3,000 km) through Alaska before emptying into the Bering Sea. Of all American rivers, the Yukon ranks third by length, fifth by volume.

Alaska has five thousand glaciers—only Greenland and Antarctica have more. North America's largest, the Malaspina Glacier near Yakutat, is larger than Rhode Island.

The northernmost state may feature vast tracts of snow and ice, but it is not frozen in space. Indeed, from a geological perspective, few regions of the world are more active. Located on the circum-Pacific Ring of Fire, Alaska is the site of a battle between the colliding Pacific and North American plates. Indeed, it is this conflict that accounts for the unusual height of Alaska's mountain ranges. As a result of this ongoing collision, forty-one of the state's volcanoes have erupted since 1700, some more than twenty times. One-quarter of all earthquake energy released in the world since the turn of the century has been released by Alaskan earthquakes.

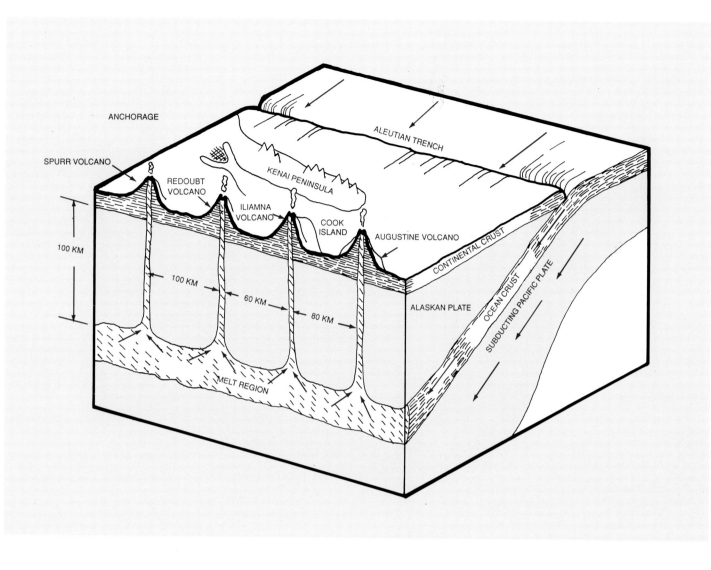

ANCHORAGE

SPURR VOLCANO

REDOUBT VOLCANO

KENAI PENINSULA

ALEUTIAN TRENCH

ILIAMNA VOLCANO

COOK ISLAND

AUGUSTINE VOLCANO

CONTINENTAL CRUST

100 KM

100 KM

60 KM

80 KM

ALASKAN PLATE

OCEAN CRUST

SUBDUCTING PACIFIC PLATE

MELT REGION

THE PACIFIC OCEANIC *plate subducts under southern Alaska at the Aleutian Trench. This diagram shows the positions of the volcanoes that result from the collisions of plates below the earth's surface.*

17

Geology

The geological forces that shaped western Canada and the western United States also created Alaska. The Coast ranges of Southeast and the Chugach, Wrangell, Alaska, and Aleutian ranges are extensions of the Cascade Mountains and Sierra Nevada to the south. The Brooks Range is the northern extension of the Rocky Mountains, which in turn is part of the great Cordillera extending north from Tierra del Fuego at the southern tip of South America. The north slope of the Brooks Range consists of limestones and shales, petroleum-bearing sedimentary rocks similar to those found on the east slopes of the Rockies.

The earth's crust is divided into huge plates that constantly shift—these are known as tectonic plates. Alaska's mountains, like the ranges of the western United States, resulted from the collision of the North American with the Pacific tectonic plates. The Pacific Plate creeps north

and west relative to the North American. The leading edge of the Pacific Plate is heated as it dives (subducts) under the North American, which in turn is thrust upward. This collision accounts for the active faults and volcanoes. Those lands closest to the plate boundaries are subject to the greatest disturbances.

If one plate were sliding past or even slightly under the other, there would be considerable activity. Along the northern Gulf, however, the North American Plate begins jutting increasingly westward. The resultant collision puts even more pressure on the boundary and results in an unusually high frequency and intensity of earthquakes in Southcentral Alaska and adjacent regions. Currently, Alaska's most active system is the Fairweather–St. Elias–Chugach Fault, which describes an arc from just west of Sitka, north of Yakutat, south of Cordova, across Montague Island, and probably across Kodiak. The concentric

MOUNT McKINLEY, OR *Denali ("the Great One"), the highest peak in North America, towers above its neighbors in the Alaska Range. First climbed in 1913, Denali now draws hundreds of climbers each year: Less than half are successful.*

BISON HERDS INTRODUCED ON THE NORTHWEST (FAREWELL) AND
*northeast (Delta) flanks of the Alaska range have done very well—in the latter case,
much to the consternation of local farmers. Not native to Alaska, the bison were
introduced more than twenty years ago and now number more than 300 animals.*

A MALE BALD EAGLE (Haliatus leucocephalus) *perches on a favorite log outside of Homer. Though endangered in other states, Alaska's healthy bald eagle population numbers some 30,000. Subsisting mostly on fish, carrion, and garbage, bald eagles also take a certain number of sea birds and small mammals. Wildlife officials have exported dozens of young bald eagles to such places as the state of New York to replenish stocks devastated by loss of habitat and indiscriminate use of pesticides and fertilizers.*

LUPINE GROWING (Nootka lupinea) *at the base of the Chugach Mountains provides good cover for voles and sparrows and the animals that prey upon them. In a matter of decades, alder and willow will top the lupine. Eventually, spruce forest will replace this meadow.*

fault bands become progressively older and less active as one moves north.

The most active volcanoes are found in the Aleutian Range. These sit on the North American Plate approximately 200 to 300 miles (320–480 km) from the plate boundaries. At that distance, the top of the plunging or subducting plate is nearly 60 miles (100 km) below the surface and has been sufficiently heated by pressure to become molten. The plate boundary occurs at the Aleutian Trench some 100 to 200 miles off the Kenai Peninsula.

All this mountain building has a payoff. Over the past billion years, mountain building and erosion have delivered valuable mineral deposits to the surface. The gold strikes of Juneau, Nome, and Canada's Klondike have had a major influence on Alaskan and American history. The Kennicott copper mine in the Wrangell Mountains was probably the richest copper deposit ever found. Even today, gold mining continues to shape the Alaskan landscape. Lead, zinc, platinum, chromium, copper, nickel, barite, molybdenum, and silver mines are either in production or development. The biggest impediments to further development continue to be high transportation costs and a depressed world market.

Climate

Alaska has four major climatic zones: maritime, transition, continental, and arctic. Within these broad zones, geography, topography, orientation or exposure, and other factors make for significantly different local microclimates.

Southeast, southern Southcentral, and the Aleutians have maritime climates, the mildest and also the wettest. The North Pacific Ocean acts as a huge thermal reservoir, warming adjacent lands during winter, cooling them during summer. Hills, mountains, and other local terrain features significantly affect the amount of precipitation. Southeast's Little Port Walter on Baranof Island is the wettest spot, with a North American record of 224 inches (560 cm) of precipitation in 1943.

The transition zone is found in the rest of Southcentral and Southwestern. As the name suggests, weather there varies between that of the maritime and the continental. Depending on distance from the coast and

DEW-BEJEWELLED WILDFLOWERS GROW ON
St. Paul Island in the Bering Sea.

FALL COMES EARLY.
Here bunchberry dogwood,
bearberry, and labrador
tea exhibit their Labor
Day plumage in Denali
National Park.

topographical influences, annual average temperatures range from 22° F (-5° C) to a few degrees above freezing.

Interior's continental climate is characterized by seasonal temperature extremes and moderate to low precipitation. In Interior, temperatures range from 100° F (38° C) in the summer to -75° F (-59° C) in the winter, and skies are generally clear. Average annual temperatures range from 15° to 25° F (-9° to -3° C).

Northernmost Alaska experiences the arctic climate. Temperatures are somewhat moderated by the Arctic Ocean, but precipitation is extremely low, with an average of 7 inches (18 cm) per year. The annual average temperature ranges from 10° to 20° F (-12° to -6° C), well below freezing.

Alaska's weather results from a combination of global wind-circulation patterns and local topography. The two biggest factors are the Aleutian Low and the Arctic High pressure systems. Relatively warm water and air south of the Aleutian Islands spawn a series of storms or low pressure systems that move eastward across the North Pacific and then progress southeastward, bringing rain and snow to Canada and the United States. A high pressure system tends to predominate over the Arctic Ocean north of the Bering Strait year-round. This system shunts storms south and east. In winter, the Arctic High can stretch over the entire state and Yukon, sending temperatures plummeting. When this weather system finally departs, the lower forty-eight states are likely to experience frigid temperatures within a few days.

Permafrost

Wherever average annual temperatures hover near or below freezing, the ground is likely to be permanently frozen—permafrost. Permafrost can be found in any type of soil or superficial deposit, even bedrock, in which temperatures have remained below freezing for many years. Except at high altitudes, permafrost is not found in Southeast Alaska and the Aleutians. On the other hand, it is virtually continuous in Arctic, Northwestern, and Western Alaska, where it can reach depths of 2,000 feet (600 m). It also extends dozens of miles seaward under the Arctic Ocean, because much of the gently sloping continental shelf was previously above sea level.

Although the surface may thaw during summer, the permafrost beneath is impermeable to surface water. The

COTTONWOOD TWINS
*on a frosty morning, late fall
in Anchorage (page 24).
Cottonwoods thrive along
river banks and on alluvial
fans, two situations where
water levels fluctuate wildly.
The tree's name derives from
the cottony fibers that carry
their seeds aloft on the winds.*

A FAVORITE WITH
*visitors to Southcentral
Alaska, the Portage Glacier
(page 25) is just south of
Girdwood on the Seward
Highway. Meltwaters drain
into Cook Inlet's
Turnagain Arm.*

THE MATANUSKA RIVER
*flows through the Chugach
mountains. Strong downriver
winds whisk loess, or glacial
silt, off the river's bars. Much
of the loess eventually settles
around Palmer and Wasilla,
creating Alaska's most
productive farmland.*

SCENE OF RAPID GLACIAL RETREAT, THE VARIOUS
*arms, inlets, and fiords of Glacier Bay are often choked
with ice like this calved off the faces of active tidewater
glaciers. Lichens, plants, and eventually forests will
grow in their wakes.*

snow-melt and rain that does not run off in rivers or evaporate remains in puddles, ponds, and lakes. This explains why the Arctic, actually one of the driest regions of the world, appears to be so wet.

In all but the coldest locales, permafrost has an "active layer" that thaws for at least a few days each year. Shading by trees and northern exposure and insulation by plants and organic mats enable permafrost to persist in areas where the annual average air temperature is now above freezing.

Permafrost presents a number of problems to northern residents. Anything that disrupts or compromises the insulating qualities of the cover can result in rapid melting of the underlying permafrost. This can have disastrous results for such overlying structures as bridges, roads, and buildings. When avoiding the permafrost altogether isn't

possible, construction strategies entail preserving the permafrost either by insulation or heat pumps. Occasionally, permafrost remnants may be thawed and the ground stabilized prior to construction.

Glaciers

Glaciers form in mountainous areas where more snow falls than melts. As layer after layer of snow accumulates, the underlying snow is gradually compressed until it becomes ice. As the ice thickens, it begins to flow downhill. Especially at its lower depths, the ice behaves like plastic. At the surface, and particularly on steeper ground, the ice will fracture like any other solid, with crevasses and seracs (pinnacles or ridges of ice) resulting.

Snow and ice can appear to be blue. They are both solids with definite crystal structures, and like other minerals, they absorb and reflect different wavelengths of light. The cleaner and denser the ice, the bluer it appears.

Alaska has three types of glaciers: alpine, valley, and piedmont. The largest glaciers are found in those parts of Southeast and Southcentral where prevailing winds bring moist marine air into contact with the soaring peaks of the Coast ranges. In some cases, alpine glaciers may literally bury the underlying peaks. The best-known examples of these are the Juneau Ice Cap and the Harding Ice Field. If the incoming snow exceeds the level of melt, the excess ice flows down into or feeds valley glaciers that excavate and occupy troughs between ridges. Some of these valley glaciers actually emerge from their valleys and spread onto the plains adjacent to the mountain range. These are piedmont glaciers, the largest of which is the Malaspina.

Glaciers advance when snow and ice accumulate faster in the upper portion than the climate can melt in the lower portion. Similarly, glaciers retreat when the upper, or accumulation, zone can not supply the lower, or melting zone, with enough ice to keep even with melting. Most Alaskan glaciers are probably in a state of dynamic equilibrium, neither advancing nor retreating much in any given year. But there are notable exceptions: Glacier Bay,

for example, is the scene of the world's most rapid glacial retreat, some 60 miles (96 km) in the last two hundred years. On the other hand, Columbia Glacier has been advancing for decades and threatens tanker traffic in Prince William Sound. Maneuvers to avoid icebergs from the Columbia were a factor in the 1989 grounding of the Exxon *Valdez*.

A large valley glacier or ice sheet can be several thousand feet thick and weigh millions of tons. Because continental crust is lighter than oceanic crust and "floats" on the earth's mantle, large accumulations of ice tend to depress the continents. When the ice melts, the unburdened land floats higher or rebounds. Rebounding rates are highest in areas that have just emerged from under the ice. Not surprisingly, Glacier Bay also has some of the highest rebound rates in the world. The land and tidelands are rising as much as 2 inches (5 cm) per year, causing major problems for the siting of boat harbors and other marine facilities. This movement is lightning fast by geologic standards, which measure time in millions of years.

Although Alaska is often associated with cold and ice, not all of the state was inundated in the Pleistocene ice ages. Indeed, much of Interior Alaska and the Yukon were ice-free. These valleys provided corridors for Asiatic people migrating into the Americas. These ice-free areas also had abundant wildlife, including many now-extinct species such as the woolly mammoth and saber-toothed tiger.

Mountains

Although parts of Alaska are characterized by expansive flats, most people associate Alaska with towering mountain ranges. Nearly all of Southeast is mountainous, and the peaks grow ever higher as one moves north towards Southcentral. The Fairweather Range, on the west side of Glacier Bay, rises abruptly from the Gulf of Alaska to 15,000 feet. Just to the north is the world's highest coastal range, the St. Elias Mountains. At 18,008 feet (5,400 m), Mount St. Elias is Alaska's second highest peak, and neighboring Mount Logan, at 19,850 feet (5,955 m), is Canada's highest and North America's second highest. Mount Fairweather is 12 miles (19 km) from the coast, Mount St. Elias, 18 miles (29 km). Even in late summer, most peaks above 6,000 feet (1,800 m) are almost completely swaddled in snow and ice. Viewed from the beach on a clear day, these ranges are unforgettable.

29

THE SOFT GLOW OF A
*winter sunset bathes Mount
McKinley and its neighboring
peaks on the south side of the
Alaska Range.*

SUNSET AND MOONRISE OVER NORTH SUICIDE PEAK,
*southeast of Anchorage in the Chugach Mountains, playground for Anchorage's
snowmachiners, skiers, hikers, dog mushers, and climbers.*

Moving north, the Coast ranges split into two branches, with the Chugach, Kenai, and Kodiak Mountains along the Gulf coast and, inland, the Wrangell, Alaska, and Aleutian ranges. The coastal offshoot is the lower of the two, with peaks generally around 7,000 feet (2,100 m). The highest peaks are found at the apex, just north of Prince William Sound, where the range curves off to the southwest. This includes 13,176-foot (3,952-m) Mount Marcus Baker. Elevations gradually decline, moving south down the Kenai Peninsula, and on Kodiak Island the highest peaks are lower than 4,000 feet (1,200 m). The traces of this range continue south, surfacing as a few widely scattered island groups.

The Aleutian Range is marked by a series of active volcanoes, many of which are covered by glaciers. In the islands west of Atka, the highest peak is 6,975-foot (2,092-m) Tanaga Volcano, and most are lower than 4,000 feet (1,200 m). Moving east, elevations gradually increase. At 9,372 feet (2,811 m), Mount Shishaldin on Unimak is the highest in the chain. The highest peaks in the entire Aleutian Range, however, rise across Cook Inlet from the Kenai Peninsula. These include Iliamna, Redoubt (which erupted throughout the winter of 1990), Spurr, and Gurdine, the highest at 12,600 feet (3,780 m). In clear weather, all four are visible from Anchorage.

The Aleutian range is connected to the Alaska Range by about 100 miles (160 km) of 5,000- to 7,000-foot (1,500- to 2,100-m) peaks. Probably the most famous of all of the state's ranges, the Alaska has two main groups of high peaks. The western group, with Mount Foraker and Mount McKinley, is by far the higher. Denali, the native name for McKinley, means "the Great One" and most who have seen the mountain agree that the Tanaina Indians knew what they were talking about. In a land of great peaks, Denali rises head and shoulders above all its neighbors. It towers more than 3,000 feet (900 m) above its highest neighbor, Mount Foraker, which the Tanaina called Denali's Wife. What makes Denali so spectacular is not just its height but its bulk. Seen from anywhere it is impressive. Perhaps the best views are from Wonder Lake, on the mountain's north flank, where it rears almost 18,000 feet (5,400 m) above a gentle plain.

The eastern Alaska Range is dominated by three peaks, Deborah, Hess, and Hayes. These peaks provide Fairbanks with a spectacular southern horizon.

To the southeast is the Wrangell Range, the state's

CLEAR DAYS AFFORD
Anchorage residents
spectacular views of the
surrounding peaks and
mountain ranges, none of
which are more dramatic than
that of Mount McKinley.

CANOEISTS ENJOY AN *early morning in late summer in Wonder Lake at Denali National Park. In the background, the shoulder of Mount McKinley and the Alaska Range.*

MOUNT KOVEN (LEFT),
Mount Silverthrone (right),
and lesser Alaska Range
summits soar above Wonder
Lake on the north side of
Denali National Park.

35

third highest, with three peaks reaching above 16,000 feet (4,800 m). Towering nearly 3 miles (5 km) above the Copper River Valley, the conical Mount Drum, Mount Blackburn, and Mount Sanford rival in beauty any of the world's better known volcanoes. The higher peaks in the Aleutian–Alaskan–Wrangell Range are heavily glaciated. Most are alpine and valley types, some of them spectacular in size and appearance. Only a few spill out onto the surrounding plains.

Protecting the Alaskan Interior from Arctic cold and wind, the Brooks Range is Alaska's northernmost, running from the Canadian border clear across the top of the state to Cape Lisburne on Bering Strait. Although its two highest peaks, Igipak and Michelson, both rise to less than 9,000 feet (2,700 m), the name of Brooks Range is nonetheless synonymous with Alaska wilderness. Just as people come from all over the world to climb Denali in the Alaska Range, people come from all over the world to hike, hunt, ski, and camp in the Brooks Range.

Because northern Alaska is so dry, only the highest peaks in the Brooks have glaciers. The frequency and size of glaciers increase as one moves west, but even there, glaciers are small alpine types. This makes it a simple matter, relative to other Alaskan ranges, to traverse the Brooks Range from north to south or east to west on foot. The lack of timber and brush and the crystalline air make it possible to see great distances and view normally elusive species such as wolves, wolverine, and the barren-ground grizzly.

Rivers and Lakes

From its origins in British Columbia only 17 miles (27 km) from tidewater in Southeast Alaska, the mighty Yukon flows 2,300 miles (3,700 km) to dump into the Bering Sea. Although airplanes have diminished its importance, the Yukon continues to be a major transportation corridor in Interior. Each spring, barges depart from Nenana with

WATER VAPOR RISING OFF the Chilkat River near Haines condenses in the cold winter air. Spring water percolating up through the river gravels sustains unusually late runs of silver (coho) and chum (dog) salmon. These fish in turn attract the world's largest eagle gathering. In years when salmon are abundant, as many as 4,000 eagles concentrate on a four-mile (6-km) stretch of the Chilkat River.

THE POT OF GOLD AT THE end of the rainbow: Mount McKinley as reflected in Nugget Pond, Denali National Park.

fuel, food, and freight for Tanana and villages downriver. Barging is often the only practical way to transport large items, structures, and craft into those parts of Interior not on the road system. Bush residents still use the river as a highway between villages and communities, traveling by boat or snowmobile depending on the time of year. The lower 2,000 miles (3,200 km), from Whitehorse downstream, are navigable.

The Yukon's major tributaries are the Porcupine, Tanana, and Koyukuk rivers. The Canadian village of Old Crow sits on the Porcupine; Fort Yukon, a trading post established by the Hudson Bay Company in 1847, marks the Porcupine–Yukon confluence. The Tanana connects Fairbanks, Nenana, and Tanana. The Koyukuk drains the south slope of the central Brooks Range and for many years provided a trade route into that region. In addition to

serving as transportation corridors, the Yukon and many other Alaskan rivers inject, in the form of salmon runs, huge quantities of high-quality protein into otherwise lean regions.

Interior's other major river system, the Kuskokwim, drains the Alaska Range west of Denali, cuts through the Kuskokwim Mountains and enters the Bering Sea 500 miles (800 km) later just downstream from Bethel. The Kuskokwim Delta teems with fish, wildlife, and particularly migratory birds. This abundance in turn supports and explains the unusually high density of native villages in the area.

Southcentral has two major river systems. Largest and most important of these is the Susitna, which drains the south slope of the Alaska Range and flows into Cook Inlet. The Susitna and its tributaries produce large runs of red, silver, and king salmon. Although the mouth is impassible, the lower portion is navigable as far upstream as the Talkeetna. Since the completion of the Alaska railroad in 1923, the Susitna Basin has been the dominant transportation corridor between Southcentral and Interior. Today, both the railroad and the Parks Highway parallel the Susitna, linking Fairbanks with the ports of Anchorage, Seward, and Whittier.

Southcentral's other major river system is the Copper. It funnels out the Copper River Basin, slices through the Chugach Mountains, and enters the Gulf just east of Cordova. Although formerly the route of the railroad that linked the Kennicott Copper Mines with tidewater, the Copper is no longer used for transportation. However, its salmon runs support subsistence, sport, and multimillion-dollar commercial fisheries.

Most of Southeast's rivers are short and swift. Three major systems cut through the Coast ranges. The Alsek-Tatshenshini system flows out of the Yukon Territory and British Columbia and enters the Gulf of Alaska 42 miles (67 km) southeast of Yakutat. Although not navigable by large boats, the Alsek cuts through the spectacular Fairweather–St. Elias ranges and provides some of the finest wilderness rafting in North America. This system has also served as a transportation and migration corridor for Native Americans and local wildlife.

The Taku snakes out of northern British Columbia and enters tidewater just south of Juneau, Alaska's capital. Like the Alsek, the Tatshenshini is not navigable, except by jet boats. However, both of these rivers do support major salmon runs.

Of the three rivers that breach the Coast ranges, only the Stikine is navigable. Earlier in this century, paddle-wheelers churned their way upstream from Wrangell 180 miles (290 km) to Telegraph Creek, an important jumping-off point for gold miners in British Columbia. Today, trappers and fishermen share the river with wilderness recreationists.

With some three million, Alaska has no shortage of lakes. Iliamna, the second largest freshwater lake in the United States, is supposedly named after a mythical, monstrous black fish. During storms, Iliamna's waves make for very rough seas. Iliamna supports large runs of sockeye salmon as do many of the other lakes in southern Alaska. Sockeyes can spawn in lakes or rivers, but their fingerlings spend the winter in lakes.

SUNSET OVER THE
*waters of "the inside passage,"
north of Sitka.*

38

MIDNIGHT SUN — MIDDAY NIGHT

Alaska's weather is closely related to annual changes in solar radiation. At the Arctic Circle, the sun remains above the horizon for twenty-four hours on the summer solstice (June 21 or 22) and below the horizon for twenty-four hours during the winter solstice (December 21 or 22). At Barrow, Alaska's northernmost community, the sun never sets for eighty-five days during the summer and never rises for sixty-seven days during the winter.

Ecosystems

At least twelve terrestrial and seven marine ecosystem types have been identified in Alaska. Taken together their names convey a picture of the state.

Terrestrial Ecosystem Type	% of total state
Glaciers and Ice Fields	4%
Lakes	1%
Riverine	2%
Moist Tundra*	17%
Wet Tundra	9%
Alpine Tundra	23%
High Brush	5%
Coastal Forest (Western hemlock–Sitka spruce)	6%
Bottomland Forest (Spruce–Poplar)	5%
Upland Forest (Spruce–Hardwood)	17%
Lowland Forest (Spruce–Hardwood)	9%
Low Brush, Muskeg-Bog	3%

*Tundra is ground cover consisting of low plants, shrubs, and mosses, frequently underlain by permafrost, and found between the tree line and the lands of permanent snow and ice.

Marine Ecosystem Type	Description/Features
Continental Shelf	Offshore to 660 feet (200 m)
Wave-Beaten Coast	Fronting Gulf of Alaska
Fiord Estuaries	Southeast, Southcentral
Tide-Mixed Estuaries	Cook Inlet
Ice-Affected Coast (Bering)	Ice in winter and spring only
Ice-Affected Coast (Arctic)	Ice may be offshore year-round
Oceanic	Over 660 feet (200 m) deep; unproductive except in Arctic Ocean

OFFERING PERCHES FOR *bird and bee, reindeer antlers poke above the wind-dwarfed lupine of St. Paul Island in the middle of the Bering Sea more than 250 miles (625 km) from the mainland.*

A FAVORITE STOP FOR
*summer visitors to Fairbanks,
the University of Alaska
Experimental Agriculture
Station boasts acres of color.*

43

A LATE SUMMER VIEW OF SCOTT PEAK AND THE POLYCHROME PASS
*country near Eielson Visitor Center, Denali National Park. Lack of tree cover, shallow
soils, and intermittent permafrost add up to rapidly fluctuating water levels in Alaska
Range rivers such as the one in the foreground.*

Forests

Southeast's forest marks the northern end of Pacific Northwest coastal forests. These are the state's most commercially valuable forests. The dominant species are Sitka spruce and Western hemlock. Red and yellow cedar are found in the southwestern part of the region where temperatures are milder. Black cottonwoods line mainland rivers and alluvial fans. Rivers like the Stikine, Taku, and Chilkat, which flow out of Canada through the Coast Range, often have stands of paper birch, lodgepole pine, and white spruce that have invaded from the Interior.

Ideal conditions in Southcentral can produce 100-foot- (30-m-) tall Sitka spruce with diameters of 3 feet (90 cm). Inland, white spruce can obtain diameters of as much as 2 feet (60 cm) and heights of 75 feet (23 m). The latter are the preferred cabin logs in Interior: The greater the diameter, the greater the insulation.

The northern, or boreal, subarctic evergreen forest is sometimes called the Taiga. It includes all the forest types listed above, except the coastal.

Timberline ranges from 3,000 feet (900 m) in Southeast Alaska to 2,000 feet (600 m) in the Brooks Range. Above 1,000 feet (300 m) in Southeast, growth is extremely slow. Thanks to seed transport by the MacKenzie River, spruce trees are found almost all the way to the Arctic Ocean in the neighboring Yukon Territory. But in Alaska, the northern limit of timber generally follows the Continental Divide along the crest of the Brooks Range. In some cases, spruce and cottonwood have crept across the Divide and established stands a few miles down the valleys. Willows up to 10 feet (3 m) high line many of the rivers and streams flowing across the North Slope. The western limit of trees arcs from just south of Kodiak on the Aleutian Peninsula northwestward past Dillingham, and Bethel, missing the Yukon delta, to Unalakleet, Council, and Noatak, where it joins the Northern limit. The forest has not reached Nome nor Kotzebue. If the climate continues to warm, the tree limit will continue to advance, albeit slowly—by some estimates, about 100 feet (30 m) per century.

Terrestrial Animals

To many, Alaska is synonymous with wildlife, partly because it is the last place in the United States with signifi-

MOONRISE OVER THE
Chugach Range from
Anchorage, Alaska. The
combination of reflective
ground cover (snow) and lots
of moonlight in winter makes
it possible to ski and exercise
long after sunset and before
sunrise for part of each
month in Southcentral and
Interior Alaska.

BROWN BEARS ENGAGE
in a little horseplay in the
McNeil River Sanctuary.
Scientists believe that the
abundance of salmon here
makes possible such
intimacies between the
normally solitary and
territorial animals.

cant populations of wolves and grizzly bears. Development, logging, and hunting pose serious threats to the continued existence of these animals, however.

Although the Alaskan grizzly or brown bear varies widely in size and color from region to region, zoologists agree that all different races and populations are the same species. The brown bears found on Kodiak Island are the world's largest terrestrial carnivores. A large bear may stand 10 feet (3 m) at the shoulder and may weigh upwards of 1,500 pounds (675 kg). The Kodiak bears' unusually large size stems from an abundance of food in the form of salmon, vegetation, and carrion, plus a relatively mild climate.

Alaska also has a small population of polar bears. These animals spend most of their time on the pack ice, but females do come ashore to den and give birth. Though prohibited in Siberia, polar bear hunting is allowed in Alaska. Because these animals follow the pack ice and cover huge distances throughout the Arctic, Soviet zoolo-

gists worry that Alaska is "mining" Russian polar bears. Cooperative studies are under way.

Other Alaskan predators include the black bear, coyote, fox, lynx, mink, marten, weasel, and wolverine.

Alaska's two most famous prey species are probably the moose and the caribou. Both of these animals are adapted to normal Alaskan winters. However, unusually deep snow prevents the moose from reaching new sources of food and can result in many deaths from starvation. Deep snow also drives moose onto roads and railroads, and into urban areas, where the inevitable vehicular collisions generally prove fatal to the moose. Currently, moose, the largest member of the deer family, are expanding their range into new areas throughout the state.

Caribou populations fluctuate widely. Alaska has some six hundred thousand caribou, divided into four or five major herds and more than a dozen smaller herds. The largest and most famous herd is the Porcupine, which winters in northern Yukon and migrates several hundred

SYMBOL OF THE FAR NORTH, THIS BULL CARIBOU WANDERS ACROSS A FALL
*landscape in Denali National Park. Having scraped all the velvet from its antlers and
fattened up during the summer, this bull faces the rigors of the fall rut.*

THOUGH LESS COMMON than their larger wolf cousins, coyotes are found in Southeastern and Southcentral Alaska, where they prey on voles and other small mammals.

49

miles each spring onto the North Slope. Caribou subsist mainly on lichens and are constantly on the move in search of food, and to escape mosquitos, wolves, and other predators. The short growing season and harsh climate severely limit the growth of plants, and thus the number of animals that the land can support. Animals tend to utilize the most productive areas, leaving vast regions virtually devoid of wildlife.

Other important prey species include the Dall sheep, porcupine, musk ox, mountain goat, snowshoe hare, bison, and black-tail deer. Some one hundred thousand black-tail deer inhabit the old-growth forests of Southeast Alaska. They have been introduced into and thrive on Kodiak and other islands in Prince William Sound. These deer rarely weigh more than 150 pounds (68 kg) and do not thrive on the mainland, where there are wolves and the snow tends to be deeper.

51

Birds

Except in coastal areas, less than twenty species of birds are common year-round. As a result, the winter woods tend to be quiet. That begins to change starting in late March in Southeast. By May, the skies of Southcentral and Interior resound with the cries of millions of birds.

In fact, some twenty million shorebirds and waterfowl stop on the Copper River Delta each spring on their way to northern breeding grounds. Millions of geese, swans, and ducks nest each summer on Alaska's many lakes, ponds, and puddles. The biggest waterfowl nesting areas are the Yukon and Kuskokwim deltas and, north of Fairbanks, the Yukon Flats. For someone who loves the outdoors, witnessing spring migration in Alaska can be a sublime experience.

Because of its proximity to and former connection with Asia via the Bering Land Bridge, Alaska hosts visiting and breeding birds from every continent. Many of these species winter in the tropics or the southern hemisphere. For example, Arctic terns wing all the way from Antarctica, a 20,000-mile (32,000-km) roundtrip. Golden

FOUND PREDOMINANTLY IN ALASKA'S
*Southwestern and Western coastal waters, these
horned puffins live on Round Island in Bristol
Bay's Walrus Islands State Game Refuge.*

SNOWY OWLS NEST ON THE OPEN TUNDRA. WITH EACH CRASH OF THE
*lemming population, approximately every four to seven winters, they move south
in search of alternative food supplies.*

plover winter in Hawaii. All told, some 400 species have been sighted in Alaska. With some 120 million seabirds, Alaska has more than the rest of the United States.

Several factors account for Alaska's rich bird life. The coastline is long and biologically productive. Summer's long hours of daylight produce a profusion of edible plants, algae, and insects. Alaska also offers a huge diversity of relatively uncrowded and intact habitats. Perhaps most important, the lean winters hold in check the numbers of resident predators.

Fish and Shellfish

By any measure, Alaska is fishing country. In fact, Alaska's commercial fisheries produce half of the world's fish protein. Fish are vital to the subsistence economy of Alaskan villages and each year attract one hundred thousand anglers from around the world.

All five species of Pacific salmon spawn in Alaska. The largest of these, the king salmon, sometimes attains weights of 100 pounds (45 kg). The largest individuals tend to come from the Kenai River and other Cook Inlet drainages.

The silver or coho salmon, next largest, seldom exceeds 22 pounds (10 kg). Dog or chum salmon average about 9 pounds (4 kg) and are named in part because the jaw on the spawning male resembles that of a dog and also because these fish were traditionally used to feed sled dogs.

Red or sockeye salmon are wonderful red-fleshed fish that feed mostly on plankton and krill. Averaging 8 pounds (3.6 kg), reds constitute the bulk of Bristol Bay's astronomical ten million annual salmon catch.

Rarely more than 8 pounds (4 kg), pink, or humpbacked salmon, are the smallest and least valuable. They tend to spawn mostly in short coastal streams. As their flesh softens rapidly, most are canned.

Lest you think that if you've seen one king salmon you've seen them all, keep in mind that commercial fishermen are able to distinguish king salmon headed for the Copper River from those headed for the Alsek, 200 miles (320 km) down the coast. Similarly, the Tlingit Indians of Haines can readily distinguish Chilkat River from Chilkoot River sockeye, though only 10 miles (16 km) separate the two rivers.

Another favorite fish in coastal Alaska is the Pacific halibut, a flatfish that sometimes exceeds 450 pounds (200

THE OVERWHELMING
*majority of Alaska's birds migrate
south each fall. One of the exceptions,
the redpoll, sticks around to add a little
color to winter landscapes from Ketchikan to
Dillingham to Fairbanks.*

ANGLERS COME FROM ALL OVER THE WORLD TO FIND SALMON SUCH AS
these on the Brooks River in Katmai National Park.

THOUGH PROTECTED BY *federal law from all but subsistence hunting, walrus are still killed for their valuable ivory tusks.*

kg). These behemoths enter coastal waters in summer to spawn and then return to deep water each fall.

Other important Alaska sport and subsistence fish are the Arctic char, grayling, sheefish (inconnu), dolly varden, burbot, tomcod, lingcod, northern pike, rainbow trout, and steelhead.

Alaska's most famous shellfish is the king crab, which weighs up to 20 pounds (9 kg) and spans nearly 5 feet (2 m) with claws fully extended. Found from Southeast Alaska to the Arctic Ocean, these crustaceans are most abundant on the continental shelf around Kodiak and in the Bering Sea.

Dungeness, tanner, and snow crab support important fisheries. Alaska also produces some of the world's finest shrimp, prawns, octopus, scallops, clams, mussels, and abalone.

Marine Mammals

Alaska's most distinctive marine mammal is probably the walrus, with its huge ivory tusks. These animals, which can weigh over a ton (.9 metric ton), like to lounge on the pack ice. Although it is legal to kill them for food, illegal slaughter for ivory continues to take many walrus lives. In Northwest Alaska, it is not unusual to find headless carcasses on the beach.

One of the most important animals in Alaskan history is the sea otter. Unlike other marine mammals that are insulated by a thick layer of fat or blubber, sea otters are protected from the frigid water only by the world's most luxuriant fur coat. The coat is a combination of 2-to-3-inch (5-to-6-cm) guard hairs and softer, finer underfur about 1 inch (2.5 cm) long. With something like one hundred thousand hairs per square inch, the density of the otter's coat is remarkable.

Sea otters prefer rocky waters shallower than 100 feet (30 m) along the outer coast where they can dive to the bottom for crustaceans and fish. A sea otter usually tucks its food into a pocket under its arm and swims with it to the surface. One of the few animals to use tools, otters frequently will float with rocks on their stomachs against which they break open shellfish.

A voracious appetite for shellfish has earned the sea otter the enmity of some commercial fishermen. Sea otters eat an average of 25 percent of their body weight per day. Considering that large males may weigh as much as 100

pounds (45 kg) each, that can add up to a lot of seafood.

The discovery of sea otters in Alaskan waters by Vitus Bering in 1741 quickly led to an international fur rush and Russian colonization. Within one hundred years, sea otters had been almost completely extirpated throughout their entire range, from Japan to Mexico. Today, the population has recovered, to an estimated one hundred thousand.

Other marine mammals found in Alaska include the Steller sea lion, eight species of seals, porpoises, and dolphins.

Some fourteen species of whales swim in Alaskan waters. Eskimos still hunt the huge bowhead whale from *umiaks*, open longboats made from skin and wood. California gray whales swim north each summer to fatten in the rich waters of the Bering Sea and Arctic Ocean before returning to winter in Baja California. Humpback whales frequent the entire southern coast at least as far west as Kodiak. They travel to Hawaiian waters for mating, though some winter in Alaska.

Dorsal fins scything through the water, killer whales frequent the same range. Though few individuals remain, the blue whale, the world's largest animal at 100 feet (30 m) weighing up to 200 tons (180 metric tons), still frequents the Gulf of Alaska. The beluga, a small, albino, bottlenosed creature, breeds in lower Cook Inlet and Shelikof Strait and is often seen around Anchorage. One of the strangest looking of all whales is found in the Beaufort Sea; the Narwhal has a single tusk or bill that projects as far as 9 feet (3 m) straight ahead.

Aurora Borealis

The aurora borealis, or northern lights, is a spectacular phenomenon that occurs when the solar winds deliver charged particles, mostly electrons and protons, to the earth's upper atmosphere. The upper atmosphere lights up or glows just the way a fluorescent lamp lights up when an electrical current excites the gases inside. The aurora can take the form of arcs, bands, orbs, donuts, spirals, and haze. Displays can be any or all colors of the spectrum. The light waves, shimmers, and flashes across the heavens because of solar wind turbulence, the high but varying speeds at which the charged particles travel, and changes in the Earth's magnetic field. Maximum auroral activity tends to coincide with the eleven-year maximum sunspot and solar-flare activity cycle.

The northern lights have their counterparts, the aurora australis, in the southern hemisphere. However, because the northern hemisphere is tilted towards the sun and because of irregularities in the earth's magnetic field, the aurora is 20 to 30 percent brighter in the northern hemisphere. Displays in eastern Siberia, Alaska, and the northwesternmost part of Canada are probably brighter than those in Eastern Canada, Iceland, or Scandinavia.

THE PEOPLE

Alaska's first residents arrived from Asia at least thirty thousand years ago, when global sea levels were several hundred feet lower and much of what is now under the Bering Sea was dry land. As continental ice caps melted and sea levels rose, the land connection between Siberia and Alaska gradually shrank. Asia and North America were still connected by the Bering Strait Land Bridge until some five to ten thousand years ago.

At that time, drier conditions in the upper Yukon valley and other lands in the immediate rain shadow of the Coast ranges kept them from being inundated with continental ice sheets. Many of the earliest human arrivals may have kept heading east and south through Interior Alaska and into the rest of the Americas. Alaska's native populations seem to have stabilized in something like their present form some five thousand years ago. Their connections with Native Americans to the south are reflected

TLINGIT TOTEM,
Southeast Alaska.

by linguistic similarities between the Athabascan and Tlingit Indians of Alaska and the Navajo, Apache, and Kiowa Indians of the Southwest United States and a few tribes in western Oregon and northwestern California.

The native population in Alaska evolved into four distinct groups: Eskimo, Aleut, Athabascan, and Tlingit. Each of these divided into numerous subgroups.

Of all the Native Alaskans, the Eskimo have remained closest linguistically to their forebears across the Bering Strait in Siberia. In fact, the recent thawing of U.S.–Soviet relations has allowed Siberian and Alaskan Eskimos to see family members for the first time since the United States closed the border in 1947.

There are three major Eskimo languages. Inupiat is spoken in the north from Unalakleet clear across northern Canada to Greenland; Yup'ik, in the Yukon and Kuskokwim deltas; and Supiaq, by the southern or Pacific Eskimos of the Alaska Peninsula, Kodiak, and northern Gulf Coast. Within these major linguistic regions, language varies from village to village.

During winter, most Eskimo lived in semi-subterra-

nean houses or lodges made of sod and wood. During summer, they emerged and moved into conical skin-and-wood precursors of the Plains Indian tepee. Generally not nomadic, the Eskimo lived in permanent villages. Families moved seasonally to permanent fishing and hunting camps. For coastal Eskimo, the main diet consisted of bearded seal, fish, and birds. In the north, using *umiaks*, large skin boats, the Inupiat hunted the great bowhead whale and other marine mammals and birds. The inland Eskimo of the southwestern Brooks Range depended heavily on moose and caribou. Eskimo were polished storytellers and carvers. With a few important exceptions, they were unusually hospitable to strangers and visitors.

The Aleut were strictly a coastal people and probably the greatest mariners and sea hunters ever. They fished and hunted for food from *kayaks*, which came to be known in Russian times as *baidarkas*. Aleut thought nothing of paddling these extremely seaworthy skin-and-wood crafts far out into the open ocean beyond sight of land. Even before the Russians' arrival, their interisland voyages often exceeded 100 miles (160 km). Some of the earliest European explorers mistook Aleut paddlers for half-bird, half-fish creatures. Lesser artists than their Eskimo cousins, Aleut nonetheless fashioned fantastic waterproof parkas called *kamlaikas* from seal gut. They captured marine mammals by lever-launched spears. As most of their territory was not forested, Aleuts lived in excavated sod-roofed houses that the Russians called *barabaras*. Entry was by ladder through the central smoke hole.

Alaska's only predominantly nomadic group, the Athabaskans occupied Interior and Cook Inlet. Those in Interior kept on the move in search of food. Although fish runs were probably fairly reliable, moose, caribou, and other game were less dependable, and starvation was an ongoing problem. Athabaskans fashioned clothes primarily from tanned moose and caribou hides. Furs provided important protection from extreme cold. This lifestyle did not lend itself to highly developed art forms, with the exception of story telling. Athabaskans living around Cook Inlet were less nomadic because of the slightly milder climate and more abundant fish and game.

The Tlingit Indians are closely related to the Athabascans. The Tlingit are thought to have reached Southeast by migrating down coastal river valleys from adjacent portions of British Columbia. They lived in rectangular wooden houses with central fire pits. Like those of the

Aleut and Eskimo, these dwellings tended to be communal. Exceptionally large ones might house ten families. Tlingit were adept fishermen and hunters, fearless warriors, and skillful traders. They acted as middlemen between tribes far to the south and the Athabaskans of the Canadian Yukon.

Like other Native Alaskans, the Tlingit had well-defined notions of property and land ownership. Specific clans held hunting and fishing rights for specific places. All others had to go elsewhere or obtain permission. Trespassers could be killed.

Of all Native Alaskans, the Tlingit probably had the most highly developed art forms. Striking totem poles towered over their villages. Lodges were decorated with elaborate paintings or crests depicting genealogies and family histories. Although the other native peoples wove beautiful grass baskets, the Tlingit made extremely durable and fine spruce root baskets. They also made and decorated cedar bentwood boxes and large wooden cooking bowls and eating utensils. The Chilkats, among the northernmost Tlingit, wove intricately designed blankets of cedar bark and mountain-goat wool. The Tlingit were also famous for the cedar canoes they paddled into battle. However, many of these canoes may actually have been obtained from the Queen Charlotte Haida just across Dixon Entrance in Canada.

Two other native peoples were found in Southeast Alaska. A band of dissident Haida from the Queen Charlottes established a toehold on southwesternmost Prince of Wales Island just prior to the arrival of Europeans. A Canadian coastal tribe, the Tsimshian, included in their territory Annette Island, just south of Ketchikan. Somewhat similar to the Tlingit, these two tribes also had highly developed art forms. Indeed, northwest coastal tribes were among the most highly developed of any in North America, probably because the relatively mild environment was so rich in food, building materials, and fuel.

Native Alaskans have developed distinct cultures in response to their local environments. Although some of these hunter-gatherer cultures may strike casual observers as primitive, their success at flourishing in some of the planet's harshest environments suggests that the opposite is the case. Indeed, these native cultures boast sophisticated technology such as watercraft, snares, and specialized fishing gear.

When the first Europeans arrived, the Native Alaskan population totaled about 75,000. That figure would have included approximately 25,000 Aleuts, 10,000 Athabaskans, 30,000 Eskimo, and 10,000 Tlingit. Disruption, disease, persecution, and starvation in the subsequent two hundred years claimed a heavy toll, particularly among the Aleuts who number only about 8,000 today. However, in the past fifty years, conditions have gradually improved for Alaska's Natives as a whole and their population currently stands at approximately 70,000, some 16 percent of the state's total.

Today, Native Alaskans hold key jobs in almost every sector of the economy, including government, finance, and medicine. However, many still reside in remote communities and live a subsistence life-style remarkably similar to that of their ancestors. For many in rural areas, economic opportunities are virtually nil and the transition from rural to urban Alaska is fraught with difficulty and even failure. Yet, despite two and a half centuries of set-

TLINGIT TOTEM FROM Haines, Alaska.

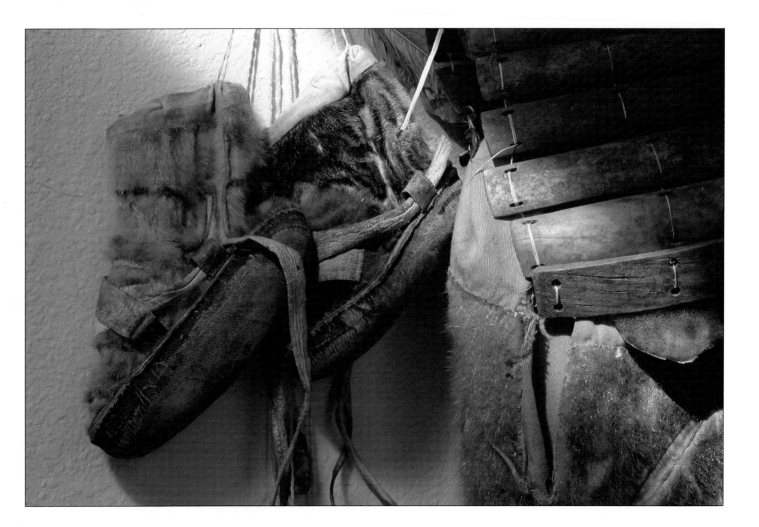

backs and frustration, Alaskan Native influence continues to grow.

In order to clear the way for the construction of the Alaska Pipeline, Congress had first to promise to resolve Native claims. When the United States purchased Alaska from Russia in 1867 for $7.2 million, the Native Alaskans and all their lands were included as part of the deal, although the tribes had never been compensated for the lands taken from them.

In 1971, Congress passed the Alaska Native Claims Settlement Act (ANCSA), which extinguished Native claims by establishing thirteen regional, four urban, and more than two hundred village corporations and conveying to these Native corporations forty-four million acres (17.5 million ha) of land and $962,500,000. While this settlement may seem extremely generous, it should be remembered that at one time the Natives controlled all 367 million acres (147 million ha) and all the resources therein. Prudhoe Bay alone may ultimately produce more than $100 billion worth of oil.

Congress intended ANCSA to encourage Native Alaskans to become part of the larger economy and capitalist system; thus, the ANCSA corporations are for-profit. As a result, the corporations have been forced into developing resources and engaging in other activities that sometimes undermine their traditional value system and culture. Today, after eighteen years, some corporations teeter on the brink of bankruptcy, through a combination of poor advice, bad investment, mismanagement, and huge attorney fees. Others are financially sound. It remains unclear how this social experiment will eventually turn out.

Early Exploration

The written history of Alaska begins with the European discovery of Alaska by Vitus Bering and Alexei Chirikof in the summer of 1741. A Dane in the service of the Russian tsar, Bering made landfall on St. Elias' day off Kayak Island 70 miles (112 km) southeast of Cordova. Sailing on a

IS THE SMILING FACE IN THE
Eskimo mask carved by George Bunyan of
Hooper Bay that of a seal or a beaver? It
has both the tree (with feather branches)
commonly associated with beavers and the
fish typically associated with seals.

The Tlingit eagle headdress of cedar and
horsehair was carved by Nathan Jackson
in the late 1970s.

Theresa Smart of Hooper Bay wove the
Eskimo grass coil basketry doll in 1987.
The doll represents a dancer wearing a
wolf mask.

different ship, Chirikof had become separated from Bering several weeks earlier. Although Chirikof made landfall to the southeast near Dixon Entrance a day earlier, Bering is more commonly credited with discovering Alaska because he was commander.

With Bering was the German naturalist Georg Wilhelm Steller. Steller did not suffer fools gladly and had made many enemies aboard before they landed. Although his relations with Bering were better than with most of the other officers, it was still all Steller could do to gain permission to go ashore. His four-hour survey on the west side of Kayak Island provided the first scientific reports on Alaska's natural history. His discoveries included the salmonberry, the Steller's jay, and the soon-to-be-extinct Steller's sea cow.

Chirikof made it back to Kamchatka, Siberia, relatively unscathed, but Bering's ship ran aground on the return in the westernmost Aleutians. Ignoring Steller's advice, Bering refused to consume the local plants, which could have cured the scurvy that killed him during the winter. Most of his men did survive, largely by eating sea otter and fashioning clothing from their furs. They pieced together enough of a boat from the wreckage of the *St. Peter* to limp back to Kamchatka the following summer. There they sold their sea-otter clothing for astronomical sums, and the Alaska fur rush began.

Europe was also racing to establish a foothold on the northwest coast. Searching for the Northwest Passage, Captain Cook reached Alaska in 1778. After making landfall and naming the Fairweather Range, he proceeded north into Prince William Sound, Cook Inlet, and Bristol Bay. At Cape Prince of Wales in the Bering Strait, having mapped much of the Alaskan coast and liberally sprinkled it with English names, he finally turned south for his fate-

ESKIMO HUNTER,
kayak, harpoon, and seal-skin
float bag to prevent quarry
from being lost. Carved from
walrus ivory, Northwestern
Alaska.

ESKIMO CHILDREN OF CHUATHBALUK FISH FOR SALMON AND WHITEFISH
in the Kuskokwim River, which serves as the major transportation route.

A NORTON BAY ESKIMO WOMAN HEFTS
*a tom cod from the hole she's cut in the ice.
Thirty seconds exposure to the cold will render
the fish as still as its brethren already at her feet.*

SYMBOL OF NEW cooperation between old antagonists, a Russian (background) and an American fishing boat ply the Bering Sea in a joint-venture fishery.

ful rendezvous with the Sandwich Islanders. Desire for fame and fur induced many of his officers to return to Alaskan waters.

Other Europeans were not far behind. The Frenchman LaPerouse entered Lituya Bay in 1786. While there, his ethnographers made the first detailed studies of the Tlingit Indians. The Spaniard Bodega y Quadra made two voyages to Southeast, reaching Kayak Island on the second. An Italian in the employ of the Spaniards, Alessandro Malaspina, in 1791 became the first European to study Yakutat Bay. By 1800, New England Yankees had made their appearance. Within four years, they were dominating a lucrative four-way trade between Alaska, China, Hawaii, and New England.

Russian entrepreneurs and *promyshleniks*, or hunters, rapidly hunted their way east along the Aleutian chains. When the Aleuts tried to resist, they were killed or captured. Using a system of captives, the Russians forced the surviving Aleuts to paddle and hunt for them. By 1784, the sea otter was virtually eliminated from the Aleutians. By the 1790s, the Russians had established posts at Unalaska and Kodiak. By 1801, under the direction of Alexander Baranof, The Russian America Company's governor general of Alaska, they had established outposts in Cook Inlet, Prince William Sound, Yakutat, and Sitka, or New Archangel, as they called it.

Each spring, flotillas of up to two hundred Aleut *baidarkas* would paddle out from Kodiak, eastward, ever eastward. As the distances grew, so too did the reluctance of the Aleuts, but they had little choice. Their sons and daughters were being held as collateral, to be ransomed annually by so many sea otter pelts. A single storm might claim half of the fleet, or 125 *baidarkas* and 250 men. In Southeast, they met stiff opposition from the Tlingit, sometimes fighting pitched battles. The Tlingit sacked and burned the invader's fort at Sitka in 1802. Two years later, the Russians retaliated, and with the help of an international bombardment drove the residents back into the forest. Eventually, the Russians leased out the Aleuts and their *baidarkas* to Englishmen and Yankees, who transported them to as yet virgin hunting grounds. By the 1830s the sea otter had been virtually eliminated from its entire range, from northern Japan to Baja California.

As the sea otter harvest declined, the Russian Court became increasingly disenchanted with its Alaskan adventure. There were, of course, individuals who suspected that

HAPPY ANGLERS LIMIT out with chicken halibut, so-called because of their relatively small size. The largest of the flatfish pictured here is probably less than seventy pounds (32 kg).

MARY LENE ESMAILKA of Kaltag hangs some Yukon River sockeye salmon out to dry. An abundance of salmon for personal consumption and dog food is crucial for residents of rural Alaska.

Alaska contained great mineral wealth and could have strategic importance, but St. Petersburg was at least six months' journey by river boat and dog sled from the Pacific and the tsar and the court were always preoccupied by things European. Needing capital to finance European adventures, Russia persuaded U.S. Secretary of State William H. Seward to purchase Alaska. In 1867, a reluctant Congress barely authorized the $7.2 million appropriation, which works out to two cents per acre.

For three decades, American interest in Alaska remained minimal. Virtually nothing was known about the interior, and few Americans had seen any of the region. True, the discovery of gold in Juneau in 1880 attracted some immigration, but it was not until 1898 that Alaska became synonymous with adventure, promise, and riches. And in fact, the event that catapulted Alaska to the forefront of national consciousness actually occurred hundreds of miles away, in Canada's Yukon Territory.

When George Carmacks and his Indian guide

Skookum Jim discovered gold on Rabbit Creek, a tributary of the Klondike River, the United States was stumbling through a depression. It was several months before word of the strike reached the outside world. But everywhere, men and women instantly dropped what they were doing to rush to the gold fields of the Klondike. Nobody bothered to tell them that the good prospects had long ago been staked. Over the next ten years prospectors fanning out from Dawson City made major discoveries near Eagle, Circle, Fairbanks, and Nome, and minor strikes in a dozen other locales.

The Yukon River had become a highway. Missionaries, educators, bootleggers, speculators, gamblers, and businessmen followed in the miners' wake. The change and abuse experienced by the Athabaskans in those ten short years are unimaginable.

As late as 1920, Alaska still had almost no roads. The highway system consisted of rivers, oceans, and winter dogsled trails. When a diphtheria outbreak threatened to

AN ESKIMO DANCER poses with her traditional summer parka and polar bear hair dance fan and headdress.

TRUE TO ITS NAME, FUR RENDEZVOUS INCLUDES OPPORTUNITIES TO BUY
furs. In recent years, animal rights organizations have used the event, commonly known
as "Rondy," as an occasion to demonstrate against hunting and trapping.

HOW MANY DOGS DOES IT take to run the Iditarod? A lot. There are at least sixty seen here in Martin Buser's dog lot at Big Lake in the Mat-Su Valley. Serious mushers may have as many as 120 dogs in their kennels.

A MUSHER GUIDES HIS TEAM ON THE YUKON RIVER, ONE OF THE RAWEST STRETCHES OF THE
1,049-mile (1,678-km) Iditarod sled dog race from Anchorage to Nome.

decimate the population of ice-bound Nome in mid-winter, serum had to be sent overland from Seward by dog sled, a distance of nearly 1,300 miles (2,080 km). That dramatic effort is now commemorated annually by the Iditarod Sled Dog Race.

In 1923, President Warren Harding drove in the golden spike at Nenana, thus signaling completion of the Alaska Railroad, which to this day connects Fairbanks and the Interior with Whittier, Seward, and Anchorage.

The advent of aircraft probably changed life in Alaska more than any other single technological development. Airplanes suddenly made it possible to cross Alaska's vast distances and huge natural barriers with relative ease and economy. Today, Alaskans fly more often and own more aircraft than any other people in the world. Alaska has almost eight times as many pilots and sixteen times as many planes per capita as any other state.

The next big event in Alaska's history was World War II. Japanese forces landed in the Aleutians in 1942 and occupied Kiska for two years before they were routed. Although the biggest enemy in the Aleutians was the weather, the "Forgotten War" saw intense battles and many casualties. Overlooked by a public preoccupied with the European and Pacific theaters, the Alaskan front may have sufficiently divided Japanese forces to result in the pivotal American victory at the Battle of Midway.

The War had long-lasting effects in Alaska. To establish a secure supply line, the U.S. War Department, in conjunction with the Canadian Armed Forces, built the Alcan Highway, which linked Fairbanks to the rest of the North American highway system. A significant number of American servicemen liked Alaska and stayed on after the war. As the Cold War intensified, Alaska experienced a second military construction boom and accompanying

AN ALASKA RAILROAD *passenger train lumbers out of the Alaska Range alongside the Nenana River just north of Denali National Park.*

HIGH-PERFORMANCE SKI-EQUIPPED LIGHT
*aircraft like this plane over the Alaska Range are the
quickest and most economical way into, and in the
case of emergencies, out of the Alaska wilderness.*

SYMBOL OF THE UNBRIDLED ALASKAN, A PAIR OF SNOWMACHINES SUMMERS
above a house in Galena on the Yukon River half way between Fairbanks and Nome.

THE $8 BILLION DOLLAR, 840-MILE (1,357-KM),
48-inch (120-cm) diameter, insulated Trans-Alaska
Pipeline snakes across Interior near Paxson. Pump
stations heat the oil and force it over four
mountain ranges.

MANY PEOPLE IN ALASKA ORIGINALLY CAME FROM
somewhere else. The state sports several licence plate trees like this one near the Kenai
Peninsula community of Sterling.

CRUDE OIL WASHES ASHORE IN PRINCE
William Sound. The grounding of the tanker Exxon
Valdez on Bligh Reef in March 1989 and subsequent
events caused Alaskans to reassess their development-
at-any-cost attitude.

improvements in the state's transportation and communications facilities.

Two closely related events ushered in modern-day Alaska. The first was the discovery of oil on the Kenai Peninsula by the Richfield Corporation in 1954. The second was President Eisenhower's signing of the Alaska Statehood Bill in 1958. Although many Americans did not know exactly where the forty-ninth state was and believed that all Alaskans lived in igloos, statehood put Alaska on an equal footing with other states.

The Alaskan economy continued to expand slowly. Then in 1968, an exploratory well produced oil at Prudhoe Bay on Alaska's North Slope, and the largest oil field in the United States was discovered. Driven by a new concern for the environment, Congress would split over the issue of whether or not a pipeline should be built to transport the oil to the ice-free port at Valdez. In 1973, Vice President Spiro Agnew, acting as senate president, would cast the deciding vote. Within a year, Alaska would experience a construction boom the likes of which it had never seen before and may never see again. The first oil flowed through the $8 billion, 800-mile- (1,280-km-)long, 48-inch- (120-cm-) diameter pipe in 1977.

At its peak in the late 1980s, about two million gallons of oil flowed through the pipeline daily.

As oil revenue started pouring into the state treasury, people from the lower forty-eight joined construction workers already in Alaska in the quest for lucrative jobs in government and industry, further swelling the state's population. The legislature perpetuated the boom by spending heavily on construction of roads, water and wastewater systems, schools, and other public facilities in practically every community in the state. Annual state

ALASKA'S LARGEST COAL mine, the Usibelli mine near Healy, supplies coal to Fairbanks, Anchorage, and Korea. The Usibelli deposits have figured prominently in the state's history. Now a symbol of the state's natural resource export-based economy, the Usibelli deposits partially motivated and fueled construction of the Alaska Railroad.

GRANARIES OF THE ALASKA FARMERS CO-OP IN DELTA. IN AN ATTEMPT TO
diversify the economy and make Alaska more self-sufficient, the legislature spent
hundreds of millions of dollars to develop an agricultural industry in Interior.
Thus far, results have been mixed.

A MATANUSKA VALLEY farm outside Palmer, at the foot of the Talkeetna Mountains. Many of these farms were developed as a result of a federal program that brought Americans of Scandinavian extraction to Alaska during the Great Depression.

spending on capital projects peaked at $2.6 billion in 1983. Plunging world oil prices in 1984 finally sent the skyrocketing economy into a tailspin. In 1990, capital spending was about $250 million per year. Some 85 percent of state revenues continue to come from the oil industry. As production begins to decline, economists forecast increasingly hard times with no relief in sight.

Fur boom, gold boom, military boom, oil boom, fish boom—Alaska has seen them all. With each bust, many people have moved on to greener fields or returned to their ancestral homes, but the population never shrinks all the way back to what it had been. And so Alaska grows by a painful process of boom and bust.

Contemporary Alaskans

Modern Alaska is a complex and varied society, with bustling cities and quiet rural settlements. Urban Alaskans work at the same types of jobs people perform in Seattle or San Francisco. Doctors, lawyers, bankers, brokers, busi-

nessmen, busboys, bureaucrats, bartenders, travel agents, janitors, secretaries, service station attendants, and other urban Alaskans live much like other people in cities elsewhere in the United States. On their days off, urban Alaskans may be found hunting, fishing, trapping, or flying off into the wilderness or halfway around the world. Some live in Alaska because they were born there, some because of economic opportunities, others because they love the great outdoors.

Residents of rural or small-town Alaska, even professionals, are even more likely than their urban cousins to derive some of their income or sustenance from the surrounding countryside through hunting or fishing.

Of all occupations, commercial fishing may be the most typically Alaskan. Alaska has dozens of commercial fisheries. In the salmon fishery alone, there are hand-trolling, power-trolling, seining, beach-seining, gill-net or drift-net, and set-net operations. These fisheries vary markedly from region to region. For example, seine boats in Southeast Alaska tend to be large, around 50 feet (15 m),

ALASKANS DON'T LET *little things like cold water prevent them from enjoying sports typically associated with more moderate climes. These sailboarders enjoy a spring day on Turnagain Arm near Girdwood, Anchorage's premier downhill ski area.*

A NATIVE ALASKAN *elder comes dressed up for the Pope's visit to Alaska in March 1981. After two centuries of exposure to missionaries, many Native Alaskans are devout Christians. Others still hold to native ways.*

A TYPICAL DAY ON THE KENAI RIVER. ANGLERS FROM AROUND THE WORLD
join Southcentral Alaskans in pursuit of feisty sockeye and the world's largest king
salmon, which reach nearly 100 pounds (45 kg).

ESKIMO WORKERS MAINTAIN a breathing hole for two California gray whales trapped off Barrow in 1988. For several weeks the whales' plight was a major preoccupation of the media and television watchers worldwide.

and target pink salmon. Prince William Sound seiners are limited to 32 feet (10 m) and target red salmon.

As recently as a decade ago, most fishermen engaged in but one or two fisheries per year. However, as technological improvements have increased fleet efficiency, seasons have become shorter and more competitive. At the same time, limited entry permits have become increasingly costly, some as much as $250,000, and fishing boats and electronics keep getting more expensive. The more a boat fishes, the faster it pays for itself. As a result, many fishermen are engaging in multiple fisheries, some of them working even eight or ten months per year.

The most successful fishermen combine shrewd business sense, mechanical expertise, nautical knowledge, and an intimate understanding of their quarry. Whether formally schooled or self-educated, these fishermen tend to be highly intelligent and politically active. Despite all the technological improvements, commercial fishing remains one of the most physically demanding, exhausting, and dangerous occupations in Alaska. Though at the mercy of almost an infinite number of factors beyond their control, such as weather, markets, and fisheries-management decisions, most commercial fishermen fish because they enjoy being on the water, working for themselves, and the possibility of a big payoff. Many rural, and particularly Native, Alaskans fish for the same reasons—but also because they have few other options.

In the 1970s, to conserve fish stocks, simplify management, and keep the size of the fleets commensurate with the resources, the state began moving to a limited entry system whereby only a certain number of permits would be issued for any given fishery. Most went to boats and fishermen already engaged in the fishery. Although the permits were free or nearly so, their value has skyrocketed in recent years. In the most lucrative fisheries, they are beyond the reach of the average person. Not surprisingly, the percentage of Natives participating in Alaska's commercial fisheries has slowly declined over the years. As fisheries in the rest of the country have declined, the percentage of nonresident fishermen has increased steadily.

IF THIS ISN'T THE *world's coldest sport, it's right up there. Snowmachiners and snowshoers encounter a slight ground-blizzard on an otherwise clear midwinter afternoon.*

GUIDES, TRAPPERS, AND PROSPECTORS

Although the North has changed a great deal since the days of Robert Service, Jack London, and Rex Beach, there are still prospectors, guides, and trappers scattered across the countryside who live much as their predecessors did nearly a century ago. The dog team may or may not have been replaced by a snow machine. The skiff or canoe may have an outboard engine. They may have traded pick and shovel for a bulldozer, there may even be an airplane parked in front of the cabin, but these individuals still survive by their wits and the resources they can scrape from the land. Their diets will often be long on moose, caribou, and salmon and short on fresh fruits and vegetables. Some will live according to the latest ecological principles; others will stop at nothing to claw the last ounce of gold from a streambed or hillside. One type of Alaskan that continues to captivate the American consciousness is the dog musher, particularly the long distance racers who compete in the thousand-plus-mile marathons: the Yukon Quest from Fairbanks to Whitehorse, and the Iditarod, from Anchorage to Nome. Once again, the old myths crumble. Some of the best of these rugged individuals are women like Susan Butcher, DeeDee Jonrowe, Roxy Wright, and Libby Riddles. Top mushers work year-round breeding, raising, and training teams. Many of the most successful Alaskan mushers live in one of several mushing hotbeds like Trapper Creek on the south side of the Alaska Range and Manley, in Interior. With their long winters, Alaskans continue to enjoy a competitive edge, but each year mushers from elsewhere continue to improve.

WINDSAILERS PREPARE *to launch their craft for a highspeed cruise of Wasilla Lake in the Matanuska Valley. In the right conditions, iceboats like these can quickly attain speeds of 50 and 60 knots.*

THE CITIES

Depending on one's perspective, Alaska's cities are like no others on earth or are strikingly similar to others elsewhere in America. Parts of downtown Juneau, for example, are reminiscent of Seattle or Berkeley. Take away the scraggly birch and white pine, and Anchorage's nicer neighborhoods look like their counterparts in Denver or Los Angeles. Anchorage's sprawl and predominance of malls and steel and glass office buildings lead some cynics to label Alaska's largest city "Los Anchorage." Many residents joke, "Anchorage isn't so bad; it's only an hour away from Alaska." But of course one cannot take away the scenery. It is the unique setting that makes each Alaskan community distinctive.

Alaska's cities tend to have that "plunked down" look, as if they'd fallen from the sky, partly because they developed as jumping-off points or outposts and partly because they tend to be surrounded by vacant or wild lands, rather than suburbs or rural areas. In fact, Alaska towns generally

PASSENGERS
disembarking at Juneau from a ferry run by the Alaska Marine Highway System make their way up a ramp steepened by low tides that can range almost twenty-five feet (8 m) in a single change. Juneau, the state capital, is accessible only by boat or airplane.

TWO BLOCKS ABOVE THE
Capitol building, fall colors blaze on Chicken Ridge, one of Juneau's oldest neighborhoods.

terminate in the bush. For example, downtown Juneau is only three or four blocks wide. In some years, black bears venture within a block of the cruise ship docks or the state capitol.

Juneau

The seat of government since 1912, Juneau is also the largest community and financial and transportation center for Southeast. The site of seasonal fish camps, Juneau blossomed overnight with the "discovery" of gold by Joe Juneau and Richard Harris in 1880; actually, the two had been led to the gold by Cowee, chief of the nearby Auke Tlingit.

By 1900, the population of Juneau and neighboring Douglas had reached nearly twenty thousand, mostly as a result of four large mines operating nearby. For a while, these were some of the largest low-grade, hard-rock gold mines in the world, but the last shut down in 1942 during a war-related national deemphasis on gold production. A battle began in 1989 over the proposed plan to reopen the A-J mine, parts of which are located less than a mile from downtown Juneau.

Today, Juneau's twenty-five thousand residents work in government, finance, tourism, fishing, and service industries. Most commute to downtown offices from the bedroom communities of Douglas and the Mendenhall Valley. Because Juneau clings to the side of a fjord, and due to its relatively small population, some residents liken it to a fishbowl. Indeed, living in Juneau for several years, it's hard to go anywhere in the immediate area without recognizing someone.

In some ways, Juneau combines the best of small-town and big-city life. Considering its size, Juneau offers a surprising number of cultural opportunities. The local professional theater presents a half-dozen plays a year.

LAND OWNERSHIP

With the passage of statehood and the Alaska Native Claims Settlement Act, the federal government agreed to convey millions of acres to state and Native ownership, thereby establishing the current land distribution pattern. The only anticipated change will be a slow transfer of a small fraction of state land to private ownership.

Owner	Acreage in millions of acres (ha)	Percent of Total
State	104.8 (42)	28.5
Federal	217.7 (87)	58.7
Native	43.7 (17)	11.9
Private	5.0 (2)	1.4
Total Acreage	367.7 (147)	100

QUITTING TIME IN
Alaska's capital. Downtown
makes for a splash of light and
color at the base of avalanche-
chute-streaked Mount Juneau.
Most city residents live in the
flat-floored Mendenhall
Valley where there is more
room for houses.

DOWNTOWN JUNEAU
*sports a fresh coat of snow on
a midwinter morning.*

Outside performers, ranging from rock to classical, give perhaps a score of concerts a year. And the town teems with visual artists and writers. Many residents participate actively in a host of civic organizations. The small size makes it possible to go fishing or skiing for part of the day, go home, clean up, and go out for the evening. Though the pace of life is decidedly slower than in larger U.S. cities, most Juneauites complain about having too much, not too little, to do.

Juneau has three seasons. Each year begins when the legislature convenes in early January. All winter, the streets bustle with lobbyists and politicians. Private jets—mostly belonging to the oil industry—are conspicuous at the airport. By the time the mandated 120-day session ends in mid-May, the first cruise ship has already tied up downtown, signaling the arrival of the second season.

The tourist season peaks in July and August when as many as four cruise ships visit each day. Streets are jammed with camera-toting pedestrians and tour buses. The harbor reverberates with floatplanes taking off, landing, taxiing, and generally making an unbelievable din. Sometimes as many as eight small planes take off in a five-minute period, most of them with a load of passengers for a forty-five minute sightseeing tour of the Juneau Ice Cap. By the time the last cruise ship slides down the channel towards Seattle on a dark and rainy night in late September, Juneau will have seen some 250 ships and 150,000 visitors.

Juneau's third season is the off season, the generally dark and rainy months of October, November, and December. During this tranquil period, indoor activities predominate. The salmon runs are pretty much over, and

103

THE OIL INDUSTRY BOOM *of the late 1970s and early 1980s brought high-rise glass office buildings to the Anchorage skyline. Like many others in the Oil Belt, the city is still recovering from the double whammy of massive over-building and a world-wide slump in oil prices.*

NO BERMUDA SHORTS *allowed. Southcentral residents work on their tans while enjoying the midway at the Anchorage Fur Rendezvous.*

most of the halibut have retreated towards the Gulf of Alaska. About a fifth of the population will venture out in pursuit of ducks and deer. The latter provide some of the healthiest, tastiest animal protein on the planet. At least until Thanksgiving, fall can be the most relaxing time of the year. Life slows down while people catch their breath after the nonstop activity of summer.

During December, while the days continue to shorten, it sometimes feels as if time has come to a standstill. The nearby Gulf of Alaska keeps temperatures at or above freezing for most of the fall, with the exception of a cold snap or two. In cold years, the real snow generally comes around Christmas and continues through February or even mid-March. However, thaws and rain are the rule at sea level. Skiers are forced to climb for reliable snow. Fortunately, the base of Eaglecrest, Juneau's municipal ski area on Douglas Island, sits at 1,500 feet (450 m). Winter temperatures seldom drop below zero, although that can feel surprisingly bitter in this damp climate. Clear, cold

weather tends to be accompanied by *takus*, shrieking winds that tumble off the ice fields east of town, gust to 80 knots, and plunge the windchill factor to -60° F (-51° C).

Anchorage

Alaska's largest city has two hundred thousand residents. If any place in Alaska deserves to be called a city, Anchorage does. Anchorage sprawls on a wedge of land between the Cook Inlet's Knik and Turnagain arms at the base of the rugged Chugach Mountains. At first glance, the backdrop to the northeast reminds one a little of Denver or Salt Lake City—but not on a clear day when Denali looms large above the northern horizon and the Alaska Range gives way to the Aleutian Range volcanoes to the southwest.

Because of its central location, port and rail facilities, and abundant flat terrain, Anchorage is the center of Alaska in almost every way: transportation, finance, law,

VISITORS ARE VIRTUALLY
guaranteed unusual lighting effects any
time the clouds part at sunrise or sunset,
thanks to Alaska's northern latitude.

A VIEW OF ANCHORAGE AS SEEN
from Westchester Lagoon.

A CABIN EMERGES FROM
the Southcentral Alaskan
mist. Spruce gradually takes
over its meadow.

108

politics, medicine, education, entertainment, culture, commerce. Three-quarters of the state's population lives within a two-hour drive. With the exception of Southeast Alaska, which has closer ties to Seattle, the rest of the state turns to Anchorage when it needs something unavailable locally.

Anchorage wasn't always so important. Indeed, the city did not exist until 1913, when construction began on a railroad that would eventually link the ice-free port of Seward with the interior. A tent camp along Ship Creek soon blossomed into a small, bustling town. With the completion of the railroad, commerce gradually increased, and Anchorage grew with it. As war threatened, Congress authorized the construction of Fort Richardson and Elmendorf Air Base. War brought an influx of military personnel and civilian construction workers. Almost immediately after World War II ended, fear of "Ivan," as Alaskans called Russia, led to a new round of military construction throughout the state. Each round swelled the local population and stimulated business. The discovery of oil on the Kenai Peninsula in 1954 and subsequently in Cook Inlet precipitated the first real growth that was not basically underwritten by the federal government. Sensing opportunity, people began trickling into Anchorage from all over the United States.

Despite the facts that only in Alaska had the enemy occupied the North American continent and that U.S. and Canadian forces were locked in a prolonged battle of hide-and-seek with the Japanese invaders, Alaska remained largely outside of national awareness until March 27, 1964. Then one of the largest earthquakes in North American history struck, completely destroying parts of Anchorage. Widespread news coverage showing dramatic images of the devastation temporarily brought Alaska to the forefront of national consciousness. With Kenai-related oil activity and the influx of federal disaster relief funds, Anchorage experienced a new construction boom and the accompanying growth. By the time that boom began to fizzle, oil was discovered 800 miles (1,280 km) to the north and Anchorage was on the brink of one of the biggest growth spurts in history.

Today, like many of its sister cities in the Sunbelt, Anchorage finds itself overbuilt and overextended. Nonetheless, provided one can make ends meet, Anchorage remains an exciting place to live. Arts and culture thrive. Some of the world's greatest musicians and dancers visit Anchorage's Performing Arts Center. The University of Alaska Anchorage's athletic teams compete regularly with the best in the nation in basketball, hockey, swimming, gymnastics, and skiing. In summer, residents can watch Alaska Baseball League games, which showcase the cream of college baseball players, many of whom become professional stars. If one prefers participating to watching, competitive and noncompetitive sport opportunities abound.

With its long days, summer is a feverish time in Anchorage. Taking advantage of direct flights from Europe and the Orient, five hundred thousand visitors from all over the world descend on Anchorage each summer. Restaurants and hotels are jammed. People never seem to sleep. The roads are almost as crowded at midnight as at midday. And in June and July it never seems to get really dark. Although temperatures rarely exceed 75° F (24° C), it's warm enough to work on a tan. Cook Inlet's 35-foot (10-m) tidal ranges are the world's second highest. The Inlet is generally too dangerous for boating so most yachtsmen moor their craft at Seward, Whittier, or Homer. However, nearby mountains, lakes, and rivers offer almost unlimited opportunities for fishing, hunting, hiking, climbing, skiing, and operating snow-machines.

Anchorage has its share of problems. Alaskans use four times as much fuel per capita as people in the rest of the United States. When the wind calms during winter cold snaps, air quality suffers. Crime, alcoholism, and drug abuse rates are among the nation's highest. The individualistic attitudes that prevail in Alaska mean that planning and zoning ordinances tend to be weaker than they might be, and may be sidestepped with variances when they prove too strong. As a result, Anchorage looks unplanned, haphazard, as if all the components fell from the sky on a windy day. Only a small part of the city has sidewalks. Commercial, residential, and industrial zones intermingle. Of course, these problems are not unique to Anchorage, or even Alaska, but in Anchorage they seem more evident and serious than elsewhere in the state. Given the spectacular setting, the results are unfortunate.

Fairbanks

Alaska's second largest city nestles in the center of Interior and serves as the commercial center for northern and northeasternmost Alaska. Birch-, aspen-, and spruce-cov-ered hills flank Fairbanks on the north, while the glacial spires of the eastern Alaska Range mark the southern horizon. Between sprawl 60 miles (96 km) of Tanana Basin flats and lowlands.

On the east, north, and west, three successive rings of sheltering hills make Fairbanks one of the most wind-free cities in the world. During the Pleistocene ice age, this meant that *loess*, or dust blown off the face of the great ice sheets, tended to settle out when it reached the vicinity of present-day Fairbanks. Today, several feet of this loess underlies much of the area. When wet, this fine material can flow like pudding. If loess contains any moisture, it undergoes significant volume changes each time it freezes or thaws. For these and other reasons, loess creates special problems for engineers and builders.

In summer, temperatures sometimes rise into the 90s (around 32° C). During winter, however, temperatures tend to stay below zero (-17° C). Temperatures of -20° to -30° F (-28° to -34° C) qualify as a cold snap, but most winters there is at least one period when the mercury plunges to 40° or 50° F below (-40° to -45° C) and stays there, sometimes for a week or two. During the coldest weather, few people venture out unless they have to.

Normally, air closest to the ground is warmest. But in places like Fairbanks in winter, the opposite is true, a condition known as inversion. Because of the stillness of the air, Fairbanks has some of the most intense inversions in the world. Temperatures may rise as much as 19° F (17° C) for every 100-foot (30-m) increase in elevation. These inversions trap pollutants and water moisture. Cold air holds much less water than warm air, so when temperatures fall below freezing, excess moisture from combustion (wood stoves, oil furnaces, vehicles) turns to ice fog. Because of the lack of wind, Fairbanks has some of the worst ice fog in the world. In really intense cold snaps, at 100 feet (30 m) straight up, the sky is clear, but at the surface, visibility may be reduced to a few dozen feet. Ice fog tends to be self-perpetuating because its upper layers reflect back incoming solar radiation and severely diminish the ability of the sun to warm air closer to the ground.

Although in many ways the residents of Fairbanks and Interior are not that different from their counterparts in other regions of the United States, their physical environment is, and it demands certain things from them. Probably one of the hardest things about living so far north is not the cold, the long summer days, nor the short

GOLDSTREAM DREDGE #8 *sits idle near Fairbanks. Placer miners opened up Interior Alaska, putting places like Eagle, Circle, Iditarod, and Fairbanks on the map. As a result of technological advances, many of the old tailings are being reworked, and quite profitably.*

113

winter days, but the constantly changing day lengths. In Fairbanks, on the winter solstice, the sun creeps above the horizon for two hours and eleven minutes. On the longest day of the year, the sun is above the horizon for more than nineteen hours and so close to the horizon for most of the remaining four that it is light enough outside to read a book.

That means that in the six months between each solstice the days have to lengthen or shorten by more than 1,000 minutes. Even if the change was constant, it would mean that each day would be more than five minutes longer or shorter than the previous. But the rate of change is not constant. As the solstices approach the rate of change slows. Therefore, around the equinoxes when day and night are approximately of equal duration, the amount of daylight is changing by nine minutes per day or more than an hour per week. This change is difficult to

keep up with, particularly for those whose ancestors lived for generations much closer to the equator.

Throw in a few billion mosquitoes and any reasonable person might begin to wonder why anyone would want to live in Fairbanks.

The answer initially was gold. Its discovery in 1901 is credited to Felix Pedro, an Italian immigrant, one of many prospectors who had fanned out into Interior in the wake of the Klondike Rush. By coincidence, Pedro's discovery was close to the head of navigation on the Tanana and Chena rivers, where E.T. Barnette had just established a trading post. Skeptics claim the discovery was a hoax perpetrated by Barnette to assure the success of his venture.

Fairbanks quickly grew into a commercial hub for Fox, Ester, and a number of other nearby mining districts. The 1923 completion of the Alaska Railroad secured its future. No longer would residents and goods have to rely

on riverboat service during the brief summers or an arduous 400-mile (640-km) dog-sled journey to Valdez in winter. Moreover, the railroad brought coal from the Healy fields, providing a reliable and relatively inexpensive supply of fuel.

The advent of airplanes enhanced Fairbanks's position as a regional center. During World War II, Fairbanks was an important stop for pilots ferrying new aircraft from factories in the United States to its Soviet Allies. Today, the area has three major military bases. Fairbanks boomed during construction of the Trans-Alaska Pipeline System. Housing was prohibitively expensive and nearly impossible to obtain. Crime rates soared. People from nearly every walk of life dropped everything in favor of the high-paying, week-on, week-off, pipeline jobs, which included room and board. Even after increasing wages significantly, local businesses had a hard time finding workers.

After construction, Fairbanks continued to grow. Many pipeline workers stayed on, because they liked the country or the opportunities or both. The bubble burst when the state ran out of money to lavish on construction projects.

Fairbanks continued to derive part of its livelihood from servicing the mining industry. Many independent placer miners operate to the north and east. Meanwhile, the importance of tourism increases each year.

The University of Alaska's main campus and administrative center are located in College, 6 miles (10 km) from downtown Fairbanks. The five-thousand-student campus has several exceptional programs, notably in Arctic-related fields. An important part of the local economy, the University also vastly increases cultural opportunities and makes the city of seventy thousand much more liveable.

Though the weeks just after the vernal equinox and just before the autumnal equinox are the nicest, spring and fall tend to be incredibly short this close to the Arctic Circle. But any time of year, Interior's vastness lends it a

special beauty. The landscape is on the scale the great chroniclers of the north led us to expect.

Alaska's Smaller Cities

Sitka was established in 1801, four years before Lewis and Clark's momentous expedition of discovery. As capital of Russian America and center of international trade, Sitka was one of the most important cities on the Pacific for several decades. It remained the territorial capital until 1912, by which time its importance had been overshadowed by that of Juneau and its gold mines. Today, Sitka is probably the most important fishing port in Southeast.

Tucked away in the northeast corner of Prince William Sound, Valdez became important with the discovery of gold in Fairbanks, 400 miles (640 km) to the north. A rugged trail led out of town over the Thompson Pass into the Copper River basin. There are still a few people alive who made the trip by dogsled. After heavy damage by tsunamis in 1899 and 1964, the town was moved four miles to a safer location. Valdez receives more snow than any other community in the United States. During the winter of 1989–90, more than 400 inches (33 feet, or 10 m) fell, setting a new record. As the southern terminus of the Trans-Alaska Pipeline System, Valdez plays a vital role in the state economy.

The Matanuska-Susitna Valley has a number of historically important communities. In 1934, during the height of the Depression, the federal government offered to relocate farmers from Minnesota and Wisconsin to Palmer, just north of Anchorage. Several dozen families moved. Today, Matanuska Valley farms produce some of the largest vegetables found anywhere, including 40-pound (18-kg) cabbages and cauliflowers.

Kodiak, like Sitka, was an important city in Russian America. Today, thanks largely to crab, salmon, and bottom fisheries, Kodiak is one of the state's most important seaports. A decade ago, the waters around Kodiak supported a booming king crab fishery, but today, either as a result of overfishing or disease, the stocks are low.

Five hundred miles (800 km) to the southwest of Kodiak, the town of Unalaska, commonly called Dutch Harbor, on Unalaska Island, is the nation's richest commercial fishing center—despite having only two thousand five hundred residents. The main port for the Bering Sea, which produces an annual catch in excess of one billion dollars, Dutch Harbor serves six hundred vessels and forty thousand workers from all over the world. Typically, fifty

POPULAR WITH SOME because no land purchase is required, floathomes seem to offer an idyllic lifestyle. However, the accompanying garbage and sewage problems and loss of access to traditional hunting, fishing, and crabbing grounds have forced communities to limit the proliferation of floathomes by zoning ordinance.

117

AS IF THERE WAS SAFETY in numbers and warmth in proximity, the houses and businesses of austere Nome crowd together.

A BOAT MOTORS INTO Nome's harbor. When gold was discovered there in 1904, ships anchored offshore and all goods had to be lightered in through the surf onto the beach—with much attendant loss of cargo and some loss of life.

A TRAPPER'S CABIN AT Kantishna exhibits the elements of classic northern construction: small size, diminutive windows, chinked logs, and a sod roof designed to exclude the Alaska Range's snow and -50° F (-45° C) cold.

THE MOSTLY NATIVE Village of Ninilchik nestles on the shore of Cook Inlet midway between Homer and Soldotna. Residents obtain the lion's share of their income from the millions of Cook Inlet Basin king, sockeye, and silver salmon.

to one hundred vessels jam the tiny harbor at any given time, and many of these exceed 300 feet (90 m) in length. Dutch Harbor is the only community in the state currently undergoing a major boom. A number of observers worry that overfishing and overcapitalization of the fleet and onshore facilities will lead to a bust.

Bethel is the commercial, transportation, and governmental center for villages in the Yukon–Kuskokwim deltas. Approximately three thousand residents work for local government or engage in subsistence hunting and fishing activities.

Nome and Kotzebue are the two most important communities in Northwestern Alaska. Nome is the regional center for communities on Norton Sound and the Seward Peninsula. With less than three thousand residents, Nome is a mere tenth of what it was in its heyday, but gold mining is still big business at the end of the Iditarod Trail. Largely Native, Kotzebue is the transportation center for the communities around Kotzebue Sound and the Chukchi Sea. Kotzebue is popular with tourists seeking the midnight sun.

Barrow, Alaska's northernmost community, is also one of its wealthiest per capita. Governmental seat for the North Slope Borough, Barrow has collected more than a billion dollars in Prudhoe Bay oil severance taxes. Natural gas is so abundant and inexpensive that few public buildings are insulated. Nowhere in Alaska are the seasonal changes in sunlight more extreme. Barrow goes nearly sixty-seven days each winter without a sunrise, although there are twelve days of twilight during this period. In summer, the sun remains continuously above the horizon for nearly eighty-two days. Because of twilight, nearly 119 days pass without a minute of complete darkness.

One might well ask why Alaskans would willingly choose to live in a place where it doesn't get dark enough in summer to see the stars; where voracious insects can make it almost impossible to enjoy the outdoors in summer; where it can rain, snow, and blow any time of year; and where it can be so cold in winter that it's dangerous to venture out of doors. The answer will be different for each Alaskan, but the results the same. For many, it has little to do with the old joke about sourdoughs: sour on Alaska and not enough dough to leave. For many it will have something to do with the perceptions of the earliest inhabitants that in so many ways, this indeed is a great land. Maybe it has something to do with the fact that the popu-

121

THE LAND OF THE LONG shadows. Alaska's northern-most village, Barrow goes sixty-seven days each winter without seeing the sun, and eighty-seven days each summer without a sunset. In the brief period when the ice pulls back, Beaufort Sea storms sometimes gobble up acres of the community's shoreline.

PART OF THE LYNN CANAL gill-net fleet tied up at Letnikof Cove near Haines as the sun appears to set up the Chilkat River Valley. Gillnetters target sockeye, chum, and silver salmon as they approach the rivers where they will spawn.

lation is small enough that individuals have some feeling for how they fit into the larger picture.

The issue that crops up again and again in Alaska is that of conservation, particularly when someone wants to develop or extract natural resources. On the one extreme are the preservationists, those who like the place just the way it is and want to keep it that way forever—or at least until advances in science and technology will sufficiently reduce the environmental impact of development. On the other hand are the developers, those who think it is humanity's purpose to develop, build, and use nature's bounty. The majority of Alaskans may lie somewhere between these two extremes.

If one takes a look at Alaska through either a preservationist's or a developer's eyes, their perspectives become understandable. The preservationists see wilderness as an ideal state. They feel a need to protect the land, an opportunity that, if not seized, will never recur. Experience here

and elsewhere suggests that any development is likely to be accompanied by a whole array of problems, environmental and social, which in the end exceed whatever short-term benefits may accrue. Developers, on the other hand, look at the map and see a different sort of opportunity: mineral deposits to develop, forests to log, energy sources to tap, roads to build. Experience tells them that if they don't take advantage of this opportunity, someone else will. There is truth in both viewpoints, and yet they are almost irreconcilable.

For most people, regardless of their perspective, it is inconceivable that someday Alaska will ever be as built up as, say, the Eastern Seaboard of the United States. The issue is where and when to draw the line. In many cases, these decisions are influenced by factors outside most Alaskans' control, by domestic and international markets and politics. Ultimately, the future of Alaska's land and cities may be beyond the control of its people.

APPENDIX

ALASKA'S SPECIAL LANDS

National Parks, Preserves, Forests, and Monuments

American people and industry have already spoken on the broad question of development through their representatives in Congress. The most recent pronouncement was the Alaska National Interest Lands Conservation Act of 1980 (ANILCA). The U.S. Congress created or expanded fifteen National Parks, fifteen National Wildlife Refuges, twenty-six Wild and Scenic Rivers, one National Recreation Area, one National Conservation Area, and thirteen Wilderness Areas in Tongass National Forest.

This legislation followed a decade of long and bitter debate and was the major environmental accomplishment of the Carter Administration. Sometimes called the crown jewels of Alaska, the lands include representative samples of nearly every type of Alaskan landscape and habitat. In many cases, the areas protected were those with relatively little potential for large-scale development activities. In most places where conflicts existed or were anticipated, special provisions were made for ongoing or future development.

The most significant exception was the preexisting Arctic National Wildlife Range (ANWR) in northeasternmost Alaska. The Porcupine Caribou herd migrates through the ANWR each spring and fall. It contains the only wilderness on the Arctic coastal plain. Petroleum geologists believe that beneath the coastal plain may be the nation's second largest oil reserves. Prior to the Prince William Sound oil spill, odds were good that Congress would allow oil-development in ANWR. As the United States becomes increasingly depending on imported oil, Congress may feel that it has no choice but to allow oil development. However, forces opposed to oil drilling in the ANWR have become increasingly successful at documenting the widespread damage resulting from oil development at Prudhoe Bay (more than four hundred spills in 1989 alone) and in pointing out that even if the most optimistic projections prove correct, ANWR will only provide three months of oil for the United States.

Southeast's Tongass National Forest is another area where conservationists and developers are locked in combat. While ANILCA protected six million (10 million) of the forest's sixteen million (6 million ha) with wilderness designation, much of this consisted of ice, snow, and rock. Logging in the forest focuses on the highest-volume stands of old-growth timber. These stands, which took hundreds of years to mature, are the most necessary to maintain wildlife, which, in turn, is important to local economies. The timber industry employs about three thousand people in the region, more than half of whom are nonresidents. Most

property and business owners in Ketchikan and Sitka, the primary mill communities, oppose any measures that might hurt them financially. Timber reform legislation has been pending in Congress for three years.

Alaska's Special Interest lands are under the jurisdiction of four agencies, the National Park Service, Fish and Wildlife Service, National Forest Service, and Bureau of Land Management. Brief descriptions of the individual areas or the values for which they were set aside follow.

National Park Service

Aniakchak National Monument and Preserve protects one of the world's largest calderas (craters), the related successional communities, and a representative portion of the Aleutian Peninsula coastal, riverine, upland, and volcanic ecosystems. 514,000 acres (206,000 ha).

Bering Land Bridge National Preserve was established to protect a Seward Peninsula ecosystem on the migratory route between Siberia and North America. 2,547,000 acres (10,188,000 ha).

Cape Krusenstern National Monument, just north of Kotzebue, is an extensive spit of sand and gravel that contains a series of aboriginal campsites dating back at least eight thousand years. 560,000 acres (224,000 ha).

Denali National Park and Preserve (formerly Mount McKinley National Park and Preserve) is one of Alaska's three original federal parks. The area was set aside to protect North America's highest mountain and its surrounding ecosystems. In 1980, Congress more than doubled the size of Denali, the state's most popular park. Each summer, almost a quarter million visitors come from around the world to get a glimpse of the mountain and some of the park's wildlife. 5,696,000 acres (2,278,000 ha).

Gates of the Arctic National Park and Preserve was established to protect a representative portion of the ecosystems of the central Brooks Range. Famous for jagged spires and expansive tundra and taiga, the park encompasses some of the greatest wilderness left in the United States. 7,952,000 acres (3,180,800 ha).

Glacier Bay National Park and Preserve is another of Alaska's three original parks. Located in the northern panhandle of Southeast Alaska, Glacier Bay boasts some of the world's most rapid glacial retreat. Its waters teem with marine life, and the land provides a natural laboratory for studying plant succession. 3,328,000 acres (1,331,200 ha).

Katmai National Park and Preserve was established in 1918 to protect the Valley of Ten Thousand Smokes, which resulted when Mount Katmai's 1912 eruption smothered the area with up to 700 feet (210 m) of ash. Although the smokes have just about disappeared, this Alaska Peninsula park is a favorite with sports fishers and people wishing to see brown bears. 4,268,000 acres (1,707,200 ha).

Kenai Fjords National Monument occupies part of the east coast, or Gulf of Alaska side, of the Kenai Peninsula. The park consists of a series of short fjords indenting heavily glaciated highlands. The entire region is slowly sinking into the Gulf as a result of the action of the Pacific Plate. Kenai Fjords is famous for its marine life and sea-bird colonies. 567,000 acres (226,800 ha).

Klondike Gold Rush National Historic Park was founded to protect the Chilkoot Trail and the objects discarded along it. Vastly improved over Gold Rush times, the trail today is a favorite with hikers. Exhibits and restored buildings make Skagway a favorite with tourists. 10,000 acres (4,000 ha).

Kobuk Valley National Park on the south flank of the Brooks Range just east of Kotzebue Sound was established to protect some of the most important archaeological sites in the Arctic, which chronicle nearly ten thousand years of Eskimo cultural evolution. Kobuk is also known for sand dunes, 25 square miles (65 square km) of them, resulting from loess blown from the face of the continental glaciers. 1,710,000 acres (684,000 ha).

Lake Clark National Park and Preserve protects the fantastic alpine scenery of the Chigmit Mountains, the southwestern Alaska Range, and northernmost Aleutian Range across Cook Inlet from the Kenai Peninsula. In addition to two spectacular 10,000-foot (3,000-m) volcanos, Iliamna and Redoubt, the east side boasts a rugged coastline along Cook Inlet. The west side has been carved into a series of deep glacial valleys that terminate in large, stunning lakes, 3,653,000 acres (1,461,000 ha).

Noatak National Preserve protects all but the last 50 miles (80 km) of the Kobuk River, which drains the southwestern flank of the Brooks Range. Flowing through mostly treeless country, the Kobuk provides an easy route for rafters and kayakers. 6,460,000 acres (2,584,000 ha).

Sitka National Historic Park was established to preserve traces of the Russian period in Alaska. It also showcases Tlingit arts. 20 acres (8 ha).

Wrangell–St. Elias National Park and Preserve contains some of the most dazzling glacier scenery and the largest ice fields on the continent. Most of the wildlife is found along the park's borders. While the high peaks belong to mountain climbers, the Chitina Valley and historical McCarthy village attract railroad, mining, and history buffs. 12,318,000 acres (4,927,200 ha).

Yukon-Charley Rivers National Preserve protects a representative portion of Interior's intermontane country. The low mountains along the Yukon Territory border supported one of Interior's first mining districts and have been home to the Kutchin Athabaskan and their predecessors for ten thousand years. 1,713,000 acres (685,200 ha).

National Wildlife Refuges

Most of the National Wildlife Refuges in Alaska were established to protect migratory birds. Inland refuges are particularly important to nesting waterfowl and shorebirds, and support healthy populations of land animals as well. Coastal refuges also tend to have large colonies of nesting shorebirds and, often, significant populations of marine mammals. Refuge status is intended primarily to protect the habitat and does not necessarily preclude development. Indeed, refuges on the U.S. Gulf Coast and the Kenai have seen gas and oil development.

NAME OF NATIONAL WILDLIFE REFUGE	SIZE IN MILLIONS OF ACRES (HA)
Alaska Maritime	4.5 (1.8)
Alaska Peninsula	3.5 (1.4)
Arctic	18 (7.2)
Becharof	1.2 (.48)
Innoko	3.8 (1.5)
Izembek	.3 (.12)
Kanuti	1.4 (.56)
Kenai	1.9 (.76)
Kodiak	1.8 (.72)
Koyukuk	3.5 (1.4)
Nowitna	1.5 (.6)
Selawik	2.1 (.84)
Tetlin	.7 (.28)
Togiak	4.1 (1.7)
Yukon Delta	19.6 (8)
Yukon Flats	8.6 (3.5)
Statewide Total	76 (30)

SUBSISTENCE

In order to gain the acceptance of Alaska's Native and rural peoples, ANILCA had to guarantee subsistence rights. Subsistence is synonymous with traditional use; both terms refer to the taking of local resources for personal use and barter. These resources include fish, wildlife, plants, and trees for food, fuel, and clothing. The gun lobby and some hunting groups opposed the creation of large parks because of potential reductions in sport and trophy hunting opportunities. To minimize the opposition, Congress created preserves that permit hunting. Hunting is allowed in National Forests and Fish and Wildlife Refuges.

The Alaska Legislature has also made subsistence the highest priority use of Alaska's renewable resources.

INDEX